Seymour Surname

Ireland: 1600s to 1900s

From Ireland Church Records of Baptism, Marriage and Death

Comprised of Roman Catholic and Church of Ireland Records

From Counties Carlow, Cork, Kerry and Dublin City

Compiled by **Donovan Hurst**

March 1, 2012

Dedication

This work is dedicated to all of those that came before us and shaped our lives to make us the people that we are today.

Table of Contents

Introduction

This is a compilation of individuals who have the surname of Seymour that lived in the country of Ireland from the 1600s to the 1900s. I have placed each entry into one of four categories: Families, Individual Births/Baptisms, Individual Burials, and Individual Marriages. If a marriage entry primarily concerns an Individual Seymour who is female, then I have placed that entry under the category of Individual Marriages. If a marriage entry primarily concerns an Individual Seymour who is male, then I have placed that entry under the category of Families. Images of many of these listings are available at http://churchrecords.irishgenealogy.ie/churchrecords/.

To help guide the reader of this work, the format of this book is as follows:

- Main Family Entry (Husband and Wife) (Father and Mother)

  - Child of Main Family Entry, including Spouse(s) when available

    - Grandchild of Main Family Entry, including Spouse(s) when available

      - Great-Grandchild of Main Family Entry, including Spouse(s) when available

(**Bolded Text**) following any entry includes any additional information such as Residence(s), Occupation(s), Signature(s), etc. when available.

Hurst

Some of the fonts used in this work symbolizes Celtic writing. The traditional letters, numbers, and punctuation marks and their Celtic counterparts are as follows:

Traditional Letters (Uppercase & Lowercase)

A a B b C c D d E f G g H h I i J j K k L l M m N n O o P p Q q R r S s T t U u V v W w X x Y y Z z

Celtic Letters (Uppercase & Lowercase)

A a B b C c D ð E e F ꝼ G g H h I i J j K k L l M m

N n O o P p Q q R ʀ S s T t U u V v W w X x Y y Z z

Traditional Numbers

1 2 3 4 5 6 7 8 9 10

Celtic Numbers

1 2 3 4 5 6 7 8 9 10

Traditional Punctuation

. , : ' " & - ( )

Celtic Punctuation

. , : ' " & - ( )

Seymour Surname Ireland: 1600s to 1900s

Parish Churches

Carlow (Church of Ireland)

Carlow Parish and Kiltennel Parish.

Cork & Ross
(Roman Catholic or RC)

Bandon Parish, Carrigaline & Templebrigid Parish, Castlehaven & Myross Parish, Clonakilty Parish, Cork - South Parish, Cork - SS. Peter & Paul Parish, Dunmanway Parish, Enniskeane & Desertserges Parish, Innishannon Parish, Kilbrittain Parish, Kilmichael Parish, Kilmurry Parish, Kilmurry, Moviddy, Kilbonane & Cannavee Parish, Rossalettiri & Kilkeraunmor (Roscarbery & Lissevard) Parish, and Tracton Abbey Parish.

Dublin (Church of Ireland)

Arbour Hill Barracks Parish, Chapelizod Parish, Clontarf Parish, Glasnevin Parish, Harold's Cross Parish, Irishtown Parish, Leeson Park Parish, North Strand Parish, Rathmines Parish, Rotunda Chapel Parish, St. Andrew Parish, St. Anne Parish, St. Audoen Parish, St. Bride Parish, St. Catherine Parish, St. George Parish, St. James Parish, St. John Parish, St. Luke Parish, St. Mark Parish, St. Mary Parish, St. Matthias Parish, St. Michan Parish, St. Nicholas Within Parish, St. Nicholas Without Parish, St. Paul Parish, St. Peter Parish, St. Stephen Parish, St. Thomas Parish, St. Werburgh Parish, and Taney Parish.

Dublin (Roman Catholic or RC)

Chapelizod Parish, Harrington Street Parish, Rathmines Parish, SS. Michael & John Parish, St. Andrew Parish, St. Audoen Parish, St. Catherine Parish, St. James Parish, St. Mary Parish, Donnybrook Parish, St. Mary, Haddington Road Parish, St. Mary, Pro Cathedral Parish, St. Michan Parish, and St. Nicholas Parish.

Kerry (Church of Ireland)

Kilcolman Parish and Tralee Parish.

Kerry (Roman Catholic or RC)

Killorglin Parish and Tralee Parish.

Families

- Andrew Seymour & Unknown

  o Henry Thomas Seymour & Georgina Mary James, b. 1851 – 15 Apr 1871 (Marriage, **Taney Parish**)

Henry Thomas Seymour (son):

  Residence - Rathgar - April 15, 1871

  Occupation - Merchant Captain - April 15, 1871

Georgina Mary James, daughter of George William James (daughter-in-law):

  Residence - Dundrum - April 15, 1871

  Age at Marriage - 20 years

George William James (father):

  Occupation - House Land Agent

Andrew Seymour (father):

  Occupation - Officer of Justice

Wedding Witnesses:

George William James & Sarah Spond

- Anthony Seymour & Elizabeth Redmond – 6 Oct 1800 (Marriage, **St. Andrew Parish** (RC))

- Bartholomew Seymour & Unknown

  o Mary Seymour & Thomas Burrowes – 27 Dec 1852 (Marriage, **St. Mary Parish**)

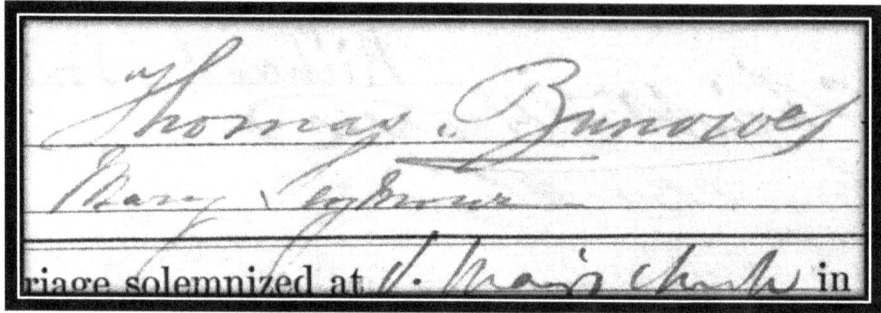

Signatures:

Mary Seymour (daughter):

    Residence - 36 Stafford Street - December 27, 1852

Thomas Burrowes, son of Peter Burrowes (son-in-law):

    Residence - 36 Stafford Street - December 27, 1852

    Occupation - Writing Clerk - December 27, 1852

Peter Burrowes (father):

    Occupation - Gentleman

Bartholomew Seymour (father):

    Occupation - Gentleman

- Charles Seymour & Elizabeth Seymour

  o Charles Seymour – bapt. 11 Jun 1838 (Baptism, **St. Audoen Parish (RC)**)

- Charles Seymour & Emilia Seymour

  o Charles Seymour & Bridget Purcell – 9 Aug 1863 (Marriage, **St. Mary, Pro Cathedral Parish (RC)**)

Charles Seymour (son):

    Residence - 41 Mabbot Street - August 9, 1863

Bridget Purcell, daughter of Thomas Purcell & Julia Purcell (daughter-in-law):

    Residence - 11 West Cumberland Street - August 9, 1863

Seymour Surname Ireland: 1600s to 1900s

- Charles Seymour & Mary Crookshank – 25 Nov 1830 (Marriage, **St. George Parish**)

Signatures:

Charles Seymour (husband):

    Residence - Londonderry now residing in Upper Rutland Street - November 25, 1830

    Occupation - Clerk - November 25, 1830

    Professional Title - Reverend

Mary Crookshank (wife):

    Residence - St. George Parish - November 25, 1830

- Charles Seymour & Sarah Jane Seymour

  - Unknown Seymour – b. 10 Dec 1874, Bapt. 14 Feb 1875 (Baptism, **Kiltennel Parish (RC)**)

Charles Seymour (father):

    Residence - Connecticut, United States - February 14, 1875

    Occupation - Shoemaker - February 14, 1875

- Charles Seymour Seymour & Catherine Seymour

  - Charles Seymour – bapt. 29 May 1831 (Baptism, **St. Mary Parish**)

Charles Seymour Seymour (father):

    Residence - 18 Britain Street - May 29, 1831

    Occupation - Servant - May 29, 1831

- Daniel Seymour & Elizabeth Leary – 20 Nov 1773 (Marriage, **Cork - SS. Peter & Paul Parish (RC)**)

- David Seymour & Bridget Egan

  - Mary Seymour – bapt. 9 Apr 1840 (Baptism, **Rossalettiri & Kilkeraunmor (Roscarbery & Lissevard) Parish (RC)**)

Hurst

- Edward Wight Seymour & Margaret Roe – 4 Jun 1822 (Marriage, **St. Peter Parish**)

Signature:

- ○ Edward Roe Seymour – b. 19 Jul 1827, bapt. 1 Sep 1827 (Baptism, **St. Peter Parish**)

- ○ Frances Elizabeth Seymour – b. 26 Aug 1828, bapt. 2 Oct 1828 (Baptism, **St. Peter Parish**)

- ○ John Hobart Wright Seymour (1ˢᵗ Marriage) & Emma Isabel Fleury – 3 Oct 1861 (Marriage, **St. Peter Parish**)

Signatures:

- ▪ Edward Michael Hobart Seymour – b. 23 Jun 1862, bapt. 19 Jul 1862 (Baptism, **St. Peter Parish**)

- ▪ Charles Marley Fleury Seymour – b. 2 Jun 1864, bapt. 7 Dec 1864 (Baptism, **St. Peter Parish**)

John Hobart Wight Seymour (son):

Residence - 4 Kildare Street - October 3, 1861

187 Lower Baggot Street - July 19, 1862

December 7, 1864

Occupation - Solicitor - October 3, 1861

July 19, 1862

December 7, 1864

Emma Isabel Fleury, daughter of Charles Marley Fleury (daughter-in-law):

    Residence - 24 Upper Leeson Street - October 3, 1861

Charles Marley Fleury (father):

    Occupation - D D

Edward Wight Seymour (father):

    Occupation - Solicitor

Wedding Witnesses:

Charles M. Fleury & E. W. Seymour

Signatures:

- John Hobart Wight Seymour (2nd Marriage) & Alice Elizabeth Parsons – 11 Dec 1874 (Marriage, St. Peter Parish)

Signatures:

John Hobart Wight Seymour (son):

    Residence - 7 Winton Road - December 11, 1874

    Occupation - Esquire - December 11, 1874

    Relationship Stats at Marriage - widow

Alice Elizabeth Parsons, daughter of Lawrence Parsons (daughter-in-law):

    Residence - Parsonstown, Kings County - December 11, 1874

Hurst

Lawrence Parsons (father):

    Occupation - Clerk of the Peber

Edward Wight Seymour (father):

    Occupation - Esquire

Wedding Witnesses:

S. W. Parsons & George Seymour

Signatures:

- o Robert George Seymour, b. 20 Aug 1836, bapt. 18 Oct 1836 (Baptism, **St. Peter Parish**) & Georgina Adelaide Birch – 1 Jun 1866 (Marriage, **St. Anne Parish**)

Signature:

Signatures (Marriage):

Seymour Surname Ireland: 1600s to 1900s

Robert George Seymour (son):

    Residence - 4 Kildare Street - June 1, 1866

    Occupation - Esquire - June 1, 1866

Georgina Adelaide Birch, daughter of William Henry Birch (daughter-in-law):

    Residence - 27 Castlewood Avenue, Rathmines - June 1, 1866

William Henry Birch (father):

    Occupation - Esquire

Edward Wight Seymour (father):

    Occupation - Solicitor

Wedding Witnesses:

S. W. Seymour & John George Birch

Signatures:

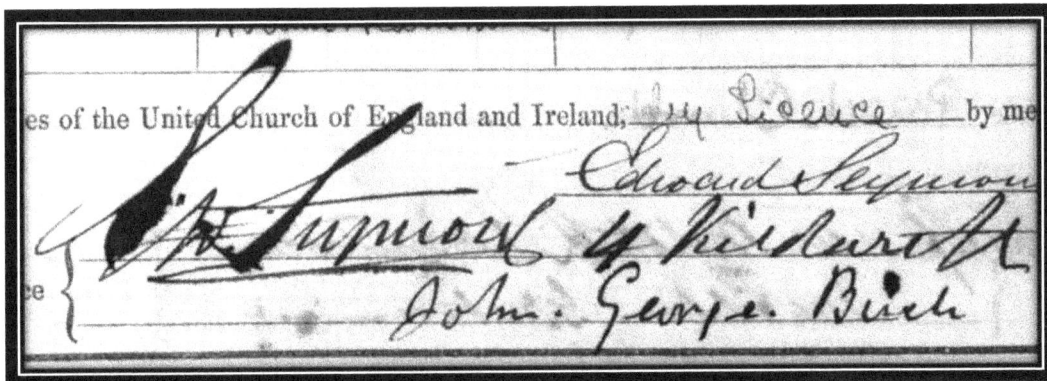

- Frances Mary Victoria Seymour, b. 11 Jan 1838, bapt. 5 Jun 1838 (Baptism, **St. Peter Parish**) & Richard Pennefather – 4 May 1872 (Marriage, **St. Anne Parish**)

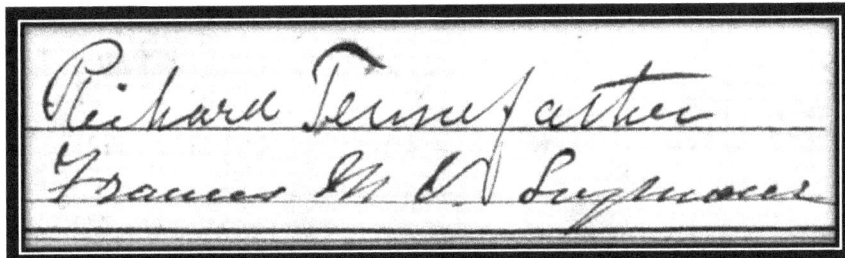

Signatures:

Frances Mary Victoria Seymour (daughter):

Residence - 4 Kildare Street - May 4, 1872

Richard Pennefather, son of Matthew Pennefather (son-in-law):

Residence - 98 Lower Leeson Street - May 4, 1872

Occupation - Esquire - May 4, 1872

Matthew Pennefather (father):

Occupation - Esquire

Edward Wight Seymour (father):

Occupation - Solicitor

Wedding Witnesses:

John W. Seymour & Robert Seymour

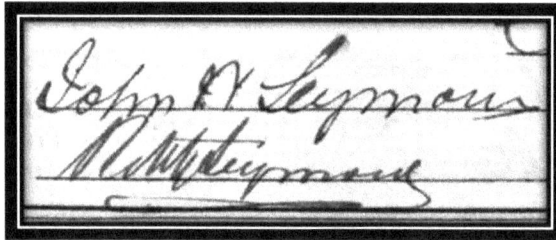

Signatures:

- o   Richard Hobart Warren Seymour – b. 13 Apr 1842, bapt. 17 Jun 1842 (Baptism, **St. Peter Parish**)

Edward Wight Seymour (father):

Residence - Baggot Street - June 5, 1838

June 17, 1842

Occupation - Solicitor - June 17, 1842

- •   Felix Seymour & Margaret Kinshinell

  - o   Anne Seymour – b. 6 Nov 1789, bapt. 6 Nov 1789 (Baptism, **Tralee Parish** (RC))

Felix Seymour (father):

Residence - Tralee - November 6, 1789

Seymour Surname Ireland: 1600s to 1900s

- Francis Seymour & Bridget Magee – 11 Feb 1795 (Marriage, **St. Michan Parish (RC)**)

  ○ Francis Seymour – bapt. 4 May 1797 (Baptism, **St. Michan Parish (RC)**)

  ○ Patrick Seymour – bapt. 16 Mar 1799 (Baptism, **St. Michan Parish (RC)**)

- Francis Seymour & Catherine Farrell Tiernan (T i e r n a n) – Jun 1781 (Marriage, **St. Michan Parish (RC)**)

  ○ George Seymour – bapt. 19 May 1782 (Baptism, **St. Michan Parish (RC)**)

  ○ Anne Seymour – bapt. 31 Jul 1783 (Baptism, **St. Michan Parish (RC)**)

  ○ Mary Seymour – bapt. 7 Oct 1784 (Baptism, **St. Michan Parish (RC)**)

  ○ William Seymour – bapt. 13 Sep 1787 (Baptism, **St. Michan Parish (RC)**)

  ○ Patrick Seymour – bapt. 12 Mar 1790 (Baptism, **St. Michan Parish (RC)**)

  ○ Catherine Seymour – bapt. 30 Jun 1793 (Baptism, **St. Michan Parish (RC)**)

Catherine Farrell Tiernan (mother):

  Relationship Status at Marriage - widow

- Francis Seymour & Unknown

  ○ Anne Seymour & Charles Unknown – 15 Feb 1766 (Marriage, **St. Werburgh Parish**)

- Francis Hugh George Seymour & Emily Mary Seymour

  ○ Hugh Delgrey Seymour – b. 22 Oct 1843, bapt. 25 Nov 1843 (Baptism, **St. Werburgh Parish**)

  ○ Florence Catherine Seymour – b. 12 Jul 1845, bapt. 13 Aug 1845 (Baptism, **St. Werburgh Parish**)

Francis Hugh George Seymour (father):

  Residence - Dublin - November 25, 1843

  Castle - August 13, 1845

  Occupation - Captain in Army - November 25, 1843

  August 13, 1845

Hurst

- George Seymour & Charlotte Lambert – 12 Oct 1841 (Marriage, **St. Thomas Parish**)

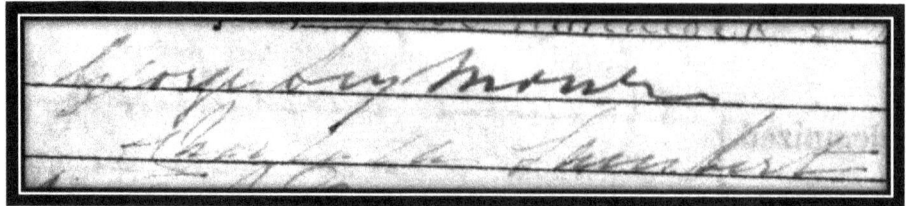

Signatures:

George Seymour (husband):

Residence - Saint Thomas Parish - October 12, 1841

Charlotte Lambert (wife):

Residence - Saint George Parish - October 12, 1841

- George Seymour & Ellen Mahony

  ○ George Seymour – bapt. 21 Mar 1820 (Baptism, **Bandon Parish (RC)**)

  ○ Edward Seymour – bapt. 7 Jan 1828 (Baptism, **Innishannon Parish (RC)**)

  ○ Mary Seymour – bapt. 28 Nov 1830 (Baptism, **Innishannon Parish (RC)**)

- George Seymour & Emily Jane Seymour

  ○ Lillian May Seymour – b. 12 Aug 1898, Bapt. 21 Sep 1898 (Baptism, **Carlow Parish (RC)**), bur. 31

    Oct 1898 (Burial, **Carlow Parish (RC)**)

Lillian May Seymour (daughter):

Residence - Barracks - October 31, 1898

   The Military Barracks Carlow, Plot 6 - October 31, 1898

Age at Death - 2 months & 17 days

   10 weeks

  ○ George Henry Seymour – b. 27 Oct 1899, Bapt. 15 Nov 1899 (Baptism, **Carlow Parish (RC)**)

Seymour Surname Ireland: 1600s to 1900s

George Seymour (father):

Residence - Barrack - September 21, 1898

November 15, 1899

Occupation - Sergt 8th K R R - September 21, 1898

November 15, 1899

- George Seymour & Jane Anne Seymour

  o George Seymour – b. 17 Mar 1854, bapt. 3 Sep 1854 (Baptism, **St. Paul Parish**)

George Seymour (father):

Residence - No **27** Barrack Street - September 3, 1854

Occupation - Laborer - September 3, 1854

- George Seymour & Julia Conlon – 4 Nov 1820 (Baptism, **Kilmurry Parish (RC)**)

- George Seymour & Mary Carthy

  o George Seymour – bapt. 9 Feb 1836 (Baptism, **Innishannon Parish (RC)**)

- George Seymour & Unknown

  o Robert Seymour & Alicia Clarke – 13 Nov 1847 (Marriage, **St. Luke Parish**)

Signatures (Marriage):

Robert Seymour (son):

> Residence - Bray - November 13, 1847

> Occupation - Merchant - November 13, 1847

Alicia Clarke, daughter of William Clarke (daughter-in-law):

> Residence - Warren Mount - November 13, 1847

William Clarke (father):

> Occupation - Merchant

George Seymour (father):

> Occupation - Merchant

Wedding Witnesses:

W. H. Clarke & William Napier

Signatures:

W. H. Clarke & William N. Trim

Signatures:

Seymour Surname Ireland: 1600s to 1900s

- George Seymour & Unknown

  o Mary Anne Seymour & William Madden – 16 Dec 1862 (Marriage, **St. Werburgh Parish**)

Signatures (Marriage):

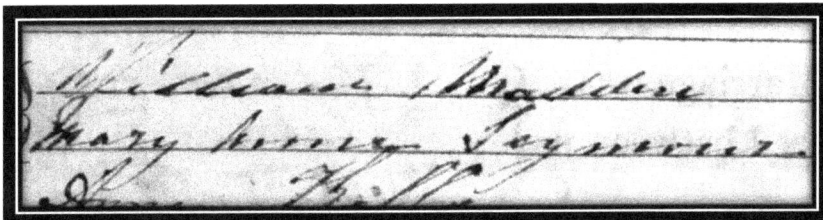

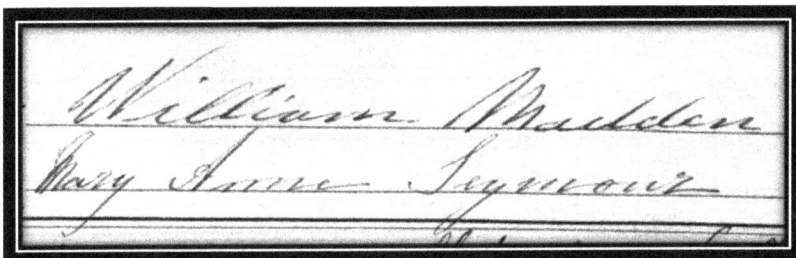

Mary Anne Seymour (daughter):

Residence - Essex Street - December 16, 1862

William Madden, son of William Madden (son-in-law):

Residence - Essex Street - December 16, 1862

Occupation - Baker - December 16, 1862

William Madden (father):

Residence - Publican

George Seymour (father):

Occupation - Servant

Hurst

- George Seymour & Unknown

  - Ellen Lambert Seymour & John Russell Stritch – 11 Jul 1868 (Marriage, **St. George Parish**)

Signatures:

Ellen Lambert (daughter):

    Residence - 6 Portland Street - July 11, 1868

John Russell Stritch, son of Andrew Russell Strich (son-in-law):

    Residence - 7 Portland Street - July 11, 1868

    Occupation - A B T C D - July 11, 1868

Andrew Russell Stritch (father):

    Occupation - Esquire R M

George Seymour (father):

    Occupation - M D

Wedding Witnesses:

Matthew M. Stritch, Frederick Taylor, & Angel T. Bond

Signatures:

Seymour Surname Ireland: 1600s to 1900s

- Gulielmo Seymour & Bridget Kinsella

  - Elizabeth Seymour – b. 23 Dec 1863, bapt. 4 Jan 1864 (Baptism, **St. Mary, Pro Cathedral Parish** (RC))

  - James Seymour – b. 14 Feb 1869, bapt. 15 Feb 1869 (Baptism, **St. Mary, Pro Cathedral Parish** (RC))

Gulielmo Seymour (father):

Residence - 70 Summer Place - January 4, 1864

21 Summer Place - February 15, 1869

- Gulielmo Seymour & Catherine Brien – 20 May 1787 (Marriage, **St. Andrew Parish** (RC))

  - Henry Seymour – bapt. 1788 (Baptism, **St. Andrew Parish** (RC))

  - Edward Seymour – bapt. 1789 (Baptism, **St. Andrew Parish** (RC))

- Gulielmo Seymour & Elizabeth Lamb

  - Mary Sophia Seymour, bapt. 1845 (Baptism, **St. Nicholas Parish** (RC)) & John Harrington – 28 Nov 1866 (Marriage, **St. Michan Parish** (RC))

    - Mary Josephine Harrington – b. 31 Mar 1868, bapt. 2 Apr 1868 (Baptism, **St. Mary, Pro Cathedral Parish** (RC))

    - William Harrington & Mary Catherine Gill – 16 Jun 1903 (Marriage, **St. Mary, Donnybrook Parish** (RC))

William Harrington (son):

Residence - Cherryfield, Rathfarnham - June 16, 1903

Mary Catherine Gill, daughter of Henry Joseph Gill & Mary Keating (daughter-in-law):

Residence - Roebuck House, Donnybrook - June 16, 1903

Mary Sophia Seymour (daughter):

Residence - Henrietta Street - November 28, 1866

John Harrington, son of John Harrington & Mary Unknown (son-in-law):

Residence - Dunlavin - November 28, 1866

51 North Great Georges Street - April 2, 1868

- Gulielmo Seymour & Marcella Keogh

  - James Seymour – b. 6 Nov 1857, bapt. 11 Nov 1857 (Baptism, **St. Audoen Parish (RC)**)

Gulielmo Seymour (father):

Residence - 54 Cook Street - November 11, 1857

- Gulielmo Seymour & Mary Johnston

  - Gulielmo Seymour – b. 28 Jan 1867, bapt. 6 Feb 1867 (Baptism, **St. Mary, Pro Cathedral Parish**

    (RC))

Gulielmo Seymour (father):

Residence - 9 Mecklenburgh Street - February 6, 1867

- Henry Seymour & Alicia Unknown

  - Agnes Seymour – bapt. 1756 (Baptism, **St. Andrew Parish (RC)**)

- Henry Seymour & Elizabeth Drought – 16 Jul 1823 (Marriage, **St. Mary Parish**)

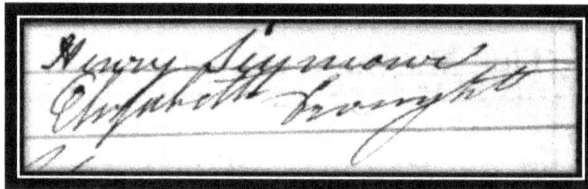

Signatures:

Henry Seymour (husband):

Residence - St. Mary's Parish - July 16, 1823

Occupation - Esquire - July 16, 1823

Seymour Surname Ireland: 1600s to 1900s

Wedding Witnesses:

Robert Drought & James Lopdell

Signatures:

- Henry Seymour & Unknown

    o   Henry Moore & Charlotte Dillon – 17 Sep 1845 (Marriage, **St. Peter Parish**)

Signatures:

Henry Moore (son):

   Residence - Julians Town - September 17, 1845

   Occupation - Clergyman - September 17, 1845

Charlotte Dillon, daughter of Charles Dillon (daughter-in-law):

   Residence - Lower Fitzwilliam Street - September 17, 1845

Charles Dillon (father):

   Occupation - Bart

Henry Seymour (father):

   Occupation - Gentleman

Wedding Witnesses:

Charles Dillon & James Joseph Mills

Signatures:

- Henry Seymour & Unknown

  - Charles Seymour & Caroline Euphemia Levinge – 19 Oct 1871 (Marriage, **St. Stephen Parish**)

Signatures:

Charles Seymour (son):

Residence - Ennis Poffey Killucan - October 19, 1871

Occupation - Esquire - October 19, 1871

Caroline Euphemia Levinge, daughter of Marc Antony Levinge (daughter-in-law):

Residence - 11 Upper Mount Street - October 19, 1871

Marc Antony Levinge (father):

Occupation - Esquire

Henry Seymour (father):

Occupation - Esquire

- James Seymour & Catherine McIlroy (M c I l r o y)

  - James Seymour – bapt. 15 May 1834 (Baptism, **St. Catherine Parish (RC)**)

Seymour Surname Ireland: 1600s to 1900s

- James Seymour & Catherine Seymour

  o James Seymour – b. 11 May 1834, bapt. 25 May 1834 (Baptism, **St. Catherine Parish**)

James Seymour (father):

Residence - Richmond Barracks - May 25, 1834

- James Seymour & Frances Dunne – 9 Jan 1831 (Marriage, **St. Andrew Parish (RC)**)

  o Mary Seymour – bapt. 1833 (Baptism, **St. Andrew Parish (RC)**)

  o Anne Seymour – bapt. 1835 (Baptism, **St. Andrew Parish (RC)**)

  o William Seymour – bapt. 1841 (Baptism, **St. Andrew Parish (RC)**)

  o Margaret Seymour – b. 1852, bapt. 1852 (Baptism, **St. Andrew Parish (RC)**)

- James Seymour & Frances Smyth

  o Catherine Seymour – bapt. 27 Jun 1849 (Baptism, **St. Nicholas Parish (RC)**)

- James Seymour & Frances Unknown

  o Mary Seymour & John Clinch – 15 Oct 1855 (Marriage, **St. Andrew Parish (RC)**)

    ▪ James Anthony Clinch – b. 1857, bapt. 1857 (Baptism, **St. Andrew Parish (RC)**)

    ▪ Joseph Christopher Clinch – b. 1858, bapt. 1858 (Baptism, **St. Andrew Parish (RC)**)

    ▪ John Thomas Clinch – b. 1861, bapt. 1861 (Baptism, **St. Andrew Parish (RC)**)

    ▪ Frances Teresa Clinch – b. 1862, bapt. 1862 (Baptism, **St. Andrew Parish (RC)**)

    ▪ John Michael Clinch – b. 19 Jan 1865, bapt. 23 Jan 1865 (Baptism, **St. Mary, Pro Cathedral Parish (RC)**)

    ▪ Mary Hannah Clinch – b. 10 May 1867, bapt. 13 May 1867 (Baptism, **St. Mary, Pro Cathedral Parish (RC)**)

    ▪ Gulielmo Clinch – b. 9 Apr 1869, bapt. 14 Apr 1869 (Baptism, **St. Mary, Pro Cathedral Parish (RC)**)

John Clinch (son-in-law):

Residence - 9 Stephen's Lane - 1858

3 Verschoyle Place - 1861

1862

108 Middle Abbey Street - January 23, 1865

39 Lower Abbey Street - May 13, 1867

112 Middle Abbey Street - April 14, 1869

- o Frances Seymour & John Fanning – 13 May 1866 (Marriage, **St. Mary, Pro Cathedral Parish (RC)**)

  - Sarah Fanning – b. 26 Jun 1867, bapt. 1 Jul 1867 (Baptism, **St. Mary, Pro Cathedral Parish (RC)**)

  - John Joseph Fanning – b. 28 Apr 1869, bapt. 6 May 1869 (Baptism, **St. Mary, Pro Cathedral Parish (RC)**)

  - Frances Teresa Fanning – b. 21 Jan 1871, bapt. 23 Jan 1871 (Baptism, **St. Mary, Pro Cathedral Parish (RC)**)

  - William C. Fanning – b. 3 Dec 1872, bapt. 16 Dec 1872 (Baptism, **St. Mary, Pro Cathedral Parish (RC)**)

  - John Christopher Fanning – b. 8 Dec 1874, bapt. 14 Dec 1874 (Baptism, **St. Mary, Pro Cathedral Parish (RC)**)

  - James Joseph Fanning – b. 7 Nov 1877, bapt. 13 Nov 1877 (Baptism, **St. Mary, Pro Cathedral Parish (RC)**)

Seymour Surname Ireland: 1600s to 1900s

Frances Seymour (daughter):

    Residence - 108 Middle Abbey Street - May 13, 1866

John Fanning, son of John Fanning & Sarah Fanning (son-in-law):

    Residence - Blessington Street - May 13, 1866

        109 Middle Abbey Street - July 1, 1867

            May 6, 1869

      108 Middle Abbey Street - January 23, 1871

      47 Middle Abbey Street - December 16, 1872

          December 14, 1874

     29 Upper Abbey Street - November 13, 1877

- Harriet Seymour & Charles Moran – 25 Jul 1869 (Marriage, **St. Mary, Pro Cathedral Parish** (RC))

  - James Moran & Anne Byrne (B y r n e) – 5 Aug 1899 (Marriage, **St. Mary, Pro Cathedral Parish** (RC))

James Moran (son):

    Residence - 108 Middle Abbey Street - August 5, 1899

Anne Byrne, daughter of Gerald Byrne & Christine Goff (daughter-in-law):

    Residence - 11 Portland Row - August 5, 1899

  - Charles Moran – b. 29 Jan 1871, bapt. 30 Jan 1871 (Baptism, **St. Mary, Pro Cathedral Parish** (RC))

  - Frances Mary Moran – b. 1872, bapt. 1872 (Baptism, **St. Andrew Parish** (RC))

  - Charles Moran – b. 30 Jan 1877, bapt. 5 Feb 1877 (Baptism, **St. Mary, Pro Cathedral Parish** (RC))

  - Mary Esther Moran – b. 12 Apr 1879, bapt. 21 Apr 1879 (Baptism, **St. Mary, Pro Cathedral Parish** (RC))

Hurst

Harriet Seymour (daughter):

Residence - 108 Middle Abbey Street - July 25, 1869

Charles Moran, son of Charles Moran & Mary Unknown (son-in-law):

Residence - 14 Fleet Street - July 25, 1869

109 Middle Abbey Street - January 30, 1871

18 Anglesea Street - 1872

15 Upper Liffey Street - February 5, 1877

44 Middle Abbey Street - April 21, 1879

- James Seymour & Margaret Kenney – 14 Aug 1756 (Marriage, **St. Andrew Parish**)

- James Seymour & Margaret Unknown

  - Frances Seymour – bapt. 25 Dec 1830 (Baptism, **St. Mary, Pro Cathedral Parish (RC)**)

- Jeremiah Seymour, b. 1785, d. 25 Dec 1847, bur. 1847 (Burial, **St. Peter Parish**) & Hannah Unknown, b. 1792, bur. 12 May 1845 (Burial, **St. Peter Parish**)

  - Samuel Steales Seymour – b. 25 May 1816, bapt. 2 Jun 1816 (Baptism, **St. Peter Parish**)

  - Robert Walker Seymour – b. 13 Jun 1819, bapt. 4 Jul 1819 (Baptism, **St. Peter Parish**)

Jeremiah Seymour (father):

Residence - Canal Street - December 25, 1847

Age at Death - 62 years

Hannah Seymour (mother):

Residence - Richmond Street - Before May 12, 1845

Age at Death - 53 years

Seymour Surname Ireland: 1600s to 1900s

- Jeremiah John Seymour & Elizabeth Sarah Seymour

Signature:

  o Hannah Seymour, b. 18 Mar 1851, bapt. 27 Apr 1851 (Baptism, **St. George Parish**) & Thomas

    Hammond – 19 Aug 1881 (Marriage, **St. Catherine Parish**)

Signatures:

Hannah Seymour (daughter):

  Residence - Rathdowney, Queen's Co. - August 19, 1881

Thomas Hammond, son of James Hammond (son-in-law):

  Residence - No 3 Clare Villa Parade Place - August 19, 1881

  Occupation - Foreman Tailor - August 19, 1881

  Relationship Status at Marriage - widow

James Hammond (father):

  Occupation - Foreman Tailor

Jeremiah John Seymour (father):

  Occupation - Bookkeeper

Wedding Witnesses:

Jeremiah Seymour & Philip Gaynor

Signatures:

○ Thomas Evans Seymour, b. 28 Sep 1852, bapt. 2 Jan 1853 (Baptism, **St. George Parish**) & Isabel Alice Lindsay – 6 Aug 1880 (Marriage, **Rathmines Parish**)

Signatures:

- Lindsay Seymour – b. 14 May 1881, bapt. 6 Jun 1881 (Baptism, **Rathmines Parish**)

- Alexander Reginald Seymour – b. 25 Nov 1882, bapt. 9 Feb 1883 (Baptism, **Rathmines Parish**)

- Iris Isabel Seymour – b. 16 Jul 1887, bapt. 23 Nov 1887 (Baptism, **St. Mary Parish**)

- Thomas Evans Seymour – b. 24 Apr 1889, bapt. 26 Jul 1889 (Baptism, **St. Mary Parish**)

- Hilda Docker Seymour – b. 14 Jul 1892, bapt. 9 Sep 1892 (Baptism, **St. Mary Parish**)

Seymour Surname Ireland: 1600s to 1900s

Thomas Evans Seymour (son):

    Residence - No 3 Clare Terrace - August 6, 1880

        25 Charleville Road - June 6, 1881

        60 Frankfort Avenue - February 9, 1883

        123 Upper Abbey Street - November 23, 1887

        123 Abbey Street - July 26, 1889

        September 9, 1892

    Occupation - Book Keeper - August 6, 1880

        November 23, 1887

        Merchant - June 6, 1881

        Accountant - February 9, 1883

        July 26, 1889

        September 9, 1892

Isabel Alice Lindsay, daughter of Alexander Lindsay (daughter-in-law):

    Residence - 15 Charleville Road - August 6, 1880

Alexander Lindsay (father):

Signature:

    Occupation - J. P. (Justice of the Peace)

Jeremiah John Seymour (father):

    Occupation - Manager

Hurst

Wedding Witnesses:

W. M. Worrall, Alex Lindsay, & H. W. G. Lindsay

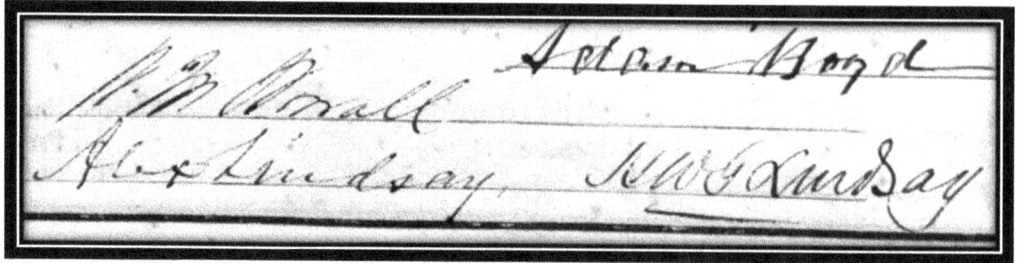

Signatures:

- ○ Frances Helena Seymour – b. 7 Nov 1873, bapt. 26 Dec 1873 (Baptism, **Harold's Cross Parish**)

Jeremiah John Seymour (father):

    Residence - 8 Villa Bank Phibsbro - April 27, 1851

                  8 Villa Bank R Canal - January 2, 1853

                  3 Clare Terrace Parnell Place - December 26, 1873

    Occupation - Shopkeeper - April 27, 1851

                  Esquire - January 2, 1853

                  Commercial Clerk - December 26, 1873

                  Manager

                  Bookkeeper

- John Seymour & Anne Farrell – 27 Jun 1806 (Marriage, **St. Mary, Pro Cathedral Parish (RC)**)

- John Seymour & Anne Lambe

  - ○ Richard Seymour – b. 12 Feb 1874, bapt. 16 Feb 1874 (Baptism, **St. Mary, Pro Cathedral Parish (RC)**)

John Seymour (father):

    Residence - 6 Ward Rotunda - February 16, 1874

- John Seymour & Charlotte Garrum (G a r r u m)

  - ○ James Seymour – bapt. 23 Oct 1825 (Baptism, **Cork - South Parish (RC)**)

Seymour Surname Ireland: 1600s to 1900s

- John Seymour & Elizabeth White – 7 May 1839 (Marriage, **St. Peter Parish**)

John Seymour (husband):

Residence - French Street - May 7, 1839

Elizabeth White (wife):

Residence - Leeson Street - May 7, 1839

- John Seymour & Frances Unknown

  o Aaron Seymour – bapt. 12 Feb 1732 (Baptism, **St. Werburgh Parish**)

John Seymour (father):

Residence - Cork Hill - February 12, 1732

- John Seymour & Grace Bransfield

  o Michael Joseph Seymour – bapt. 1 Feb 1835 (Baptism, **Cork - SS. Peter & Paul Parish (RC)**)

- John Seymour & Grace Unknown

  o Grace Caroline Seymour – bapt. 29 May 1818 (Baptism, **Clonakilty Parish (RC)**)

- John Seymour & Grizell Hubbart – 19 Oct 1761 (Marriage, **St. Anne Parish**)

John Seymour (husband):

Professional Title - Reverend

- John Seymour & Ismah Unknown, bur. 21 Jul 1690 (Burial, **St. Nicholas Within Parish**)

- John Seymour & Jane Unknown

  o Mary Seymour – bapt. 27 Feb 1731 (Baptism, **St. Michan Parish (RC)**)

  o Catherine Seymour – bapt. 28 Apr 1735 (Baptism, **St. Michan Parish (RC)**)

John Seymour (father):

Residence - Kings Street - February 27, 1731

April 28, 1735

Hurst

- John Seymour & Margaret Maddin

  ○ Margaret Seymour – bapt. 10 Jun 1801 (Baptism, **Cork - South Parish (RC)**)

John Seymour (father):

Residence - Army - June 10, 1801

- John Seymour & Margaret O'Connell – 21 Dec 1875 (Baptism, **Kilmurry, Moviddy, Kilbonane & Cannavee Parish (RC)**)

- John Seymour & Margaret Seymour

  ○ Anne Seymour – bapt. 3 Jul 1827 (Baptism, **St. Mary, Pro Cathedral Parish (RC)**)

John Seymour (father):

Residence - Bray - July 3, 1827

- John Seymour & Margaret Swiney

  ○ Margaret Seymour – bapt. 20 Sep 1829 (Baptism, **Innishannon Parish (RC)**)

- John Seymour & Mary Doyle

  ○ Thomas Seymour – bapt. 23 Dec 1804 (Baptism, **St. James Parish (RC)**)

  ○ Gulielmo Seymour – bapt. 20 Apr 1806 (Baptism, **St. James Parish (RC)**)

- John Seymour & Mary Dunne

  ○ George Seymour – bapt. 29 May 1848 (Baptism, **St. Michan Parish (RC)**)

- John Seymour & Mary Reilly – 13 Dec 1832 (Marriage, **St. Peter Parish**)

John Seymour (husband):

Residence - King Street South, St. Peter's - December 13, 1832

Mary Reilly (wife):

Residence - Kings Street South, St. Peter's - December 13, 1832

- John Seymour & Mary Seymour

  ○ John Seymour – bapt. 26 Jul 1833 (Baptism, **St. Mary, Pro Cathedral Parish (RC)**)

Seymour Surname Ireland: 1600s to 1900s

- John Seymour & Mary Seymour

  o Aiden Seymour & Mary Helen Cremen (C r e m e n) – 12 Oct 1889 (Marriage, **Killorglin Parish (RC)**)

    ▪ Honora Mary Seymour – b. 26 Jul 1890, bapt. 31 Jul 1890 (Baptism, **Killorglin Parish** (RC))

    ▪ Helen Seymour – b. 1 Sep 1893, bapt. 3 Sep 1893 (Baptism, **Killorglin Parish** (RC))

    ▪ Patrick James Seymour – b. 4 Mar 1895, bapt. 7 Mar 1895 (Baptism, **Killorglin Parish** (RC))

Aiden Seymour (son):

Residence - Killorglin - October 12, 1889

July 31, 1890

March 7, 1895

Naas - September 3, 1893

Mary Helen Cremen, daughter of Cornelius Cremen & Mary Mulcahy (daughter-in-law):

Residence - Killorglin - October 12, 1889

- John Seymour & Mary Unknown

  o Margaret Seymour – bapt. 13 Jul 1807 (Baptism, **St. Mary, Pro Cathedral Parish** (RC))

- John Seymour & Mary Unknown

  o Margaret Seymour & Joseph Dwane – 2 May 1863 (Marriage, **St. Michan Parish** (RC))

Margaret Seymour (daughter):

Residence - 1 Anne Street - May 2, 1863

Joseph Dwane, son of Joseph Dwane & Mary Unknown (son-in-law):

Residence - 91 James Street - May 2, 1863

Hurst

- John Seymour & Mary Unknown

    o John Seymour & Catherine Dunne – 15 Jun 1872 (Marriage, **St. Michan Parish (RC)**)

        ▪ Margaret Mary Seymour – b. 2 Oct 1877, bapt. 8 Oct 1877 (Baptism, **St. Mary, Haddington Road Parish (RC)**)

        ▪ Joseph Michael Seymour – b. 28 Mar 1879, bapt. 14 Apr 1879 (Baptism, **St. Mary, Haddington Road Parish (RC)**)

John Seymour (son):

Residence - 1 North Anne Street - June 15, 1872

43 Bath Avenue - October 8, 1877

April 14, 1879

Catherine Dunne, daughter of Patrick Dunne & Mary Unknown (daughter-in-law):

Residence - 78 Upper Dominick Street - June 15, 1872

- John Seymour & Mary Unknown

    o George Seymour & Catherine Dunne – 4 Aug 1872 (Marriage, **St. Andrew Parish (RC)**)

        ▪ George Patrick Seymour – b. 1873, bapt. 1873 (Baptism, **St. Andrew Parish (RC)**)

        ▪ John Seymour – b. 1875, bapt. 1875 (Baptism, **St. Andrew Parish (RC)**)

        ▪ Eva Florence Margaret Seymour – b. 1885, bapt. 1885 (Baptism, **St. Andrew Parish (RC)**)

        ▪ George Joseph Seymour – b. 1888, bapt. 1888 (Baptism, **St. Andrew Parish (RC)**)

        ▪ Mary Josephine Felicitus Seymour – b. 1890, bapt. 1890 (Baptism, **St. Andrew Parish (RC)**)

George Seymour (son):

Residence - 20 Heytesbury Street - August 4, 1872

28 Queen's Square - 1873

1875

27 Queen's Square - 1885

1888

1890

Seymour Surname Ireland: 1600s to 1900s

Catherine Dunne, daughter of George Dunne & Margaret Unknown (daughter-in-law):

>Residence - 43 Deuzille Street - August 4, 1872

Wedding Witnesses:

John Seymour & Margaret Ward

- John Seymour & Mary Walsh – 29 Nov 1844 (Marriage, **St. Catherine Parish** (RC))

    o Mary Seymour – bapt. 2 Sep 1845 (Baptism, **St. Catherine Parish** (RC))

- John Seymour & Mary Anne Jennings

    o Mary Catherine Seymour – b. 17 May 1886, bapt. 21 May 1886 (Baptism, **St. Michan Parish** (RC))

    o Josephine Nugent Seymour – b. 19 Oct 1887, bapt. 31 Oct 1887 (Baptism, **St. Michan Parish** (RC))

John Seymour (father):

>Residence - 46 Mountjoy Street - May 21, 1886

>>30 Fontenoy Street - October 31, 1887

- John Seymour & Unknown

    o Ealter Seymour – bapt. 28 Apr 1698 (Baptism, **St. Nicholas Within Parish**)

- John Seymour & Unknown

    o William Seymour & Elizabeth Hanman (H a n m a n) – 25 Jan 1853 (Marriage, **St. Anne Parish**)

Signatures:

William Seymour (son):

>Residence - 8 Upper Merrion Street - January 25, 1853

>Occupation - Servant - January 25, 1853

Elizabeth Hanman, daughter of Thomas Hanman (daughter-in-law):

>Residence - 8 Upper Merrion Street - January 25, 1853

Thomas Hanman (father):

Occupation - Servant

John Seymour (father):

Occupation - Servant

- John Seymour & Unknown

  o Peter Seymour & Mary Byrne (B y r n e) – 29 Dec 1875 (Marriage, **St. Peter Parish**)

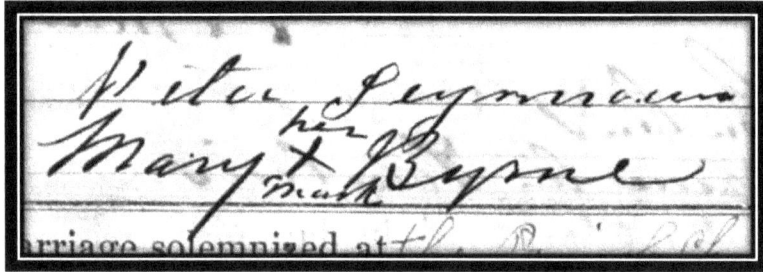

Signatures:

Peter Seymour (son):

Residence - Haddington Road - December 29, 1875

Occupation - Servant - December 29, 1875

Relationship Status at Marriage - widow

Mary Byrne, daughter of John Byrne (daughter-in-law):

Residence - Haddington Road - December 29, 1875

Relationship Status at Marriage - widow

John Byrne (father):

Occupation - Blacksmith

John Seymour (father):

Occupation - Carpenter

Seymour Surname Ireland: 1600s to 1900s

- John Seymour & Unknown

  o Elizabeth Seymour & Samuel Young – 25 Dec 1885 (Marriage, **St. Andrew Parish**)

Signatures:

  - Mary Jane Young – b. 1887, bapt. 1888 (Baptism, **St. Andrew Parish** (RC))

  - Henry Young – b. 1889, bapt. 1890 (Baptism, **St. Andrew Parish** (RC))

  - Alice Young – b. 16 Aug 1891, bapt. Aug 1891 (Baptism, **SS. Michael & John Parish** (RC))

Elizabeth Seymour (daughter):

   Residence - 1 St. Andrew Street - December 25, 1885

   Relationship Status at Marriage - minor

Samuel Young, son of Henry Young (son-in-law):

   Residence - 73 Aungier Street - December 25, 1885

                29 Wicklow Street - 1888

                18 Andrew Street - 1890

                61 George's Street - August 1891

   Occupation - Tailor - December 25, 1885

Henry Young (father):

   Occupation - House Painter

John Seymour (father):

   Occupation - Pensioner

33

Hurst

- John Seymour & Unknown

  o Elizabeth Jane Seymour & James Kirby Bervie – 6 Jan 1887 (Marriage, **Taney Parish**)

Elizabeth Jane Seymour (daughter):

Residence - 3 Campfield Terrace - January 6, 1887

James Kirby Bervie, son of Samuel Bervie (son-in-law):

Residence - 51 Raymond Street, Dublin - January 6, 1887

Occupation - Commercial Clerk - January 6, 1887

Samuel Bervie (father):

Occupation - Schoolmaster

John Seymour (father):

Occupation - Soldier

Wedding Witnesses:

John Seymour & James Doyle

- John Adam Seymour & Rebecca Grant – 9 May 1752 (Marriage, **St. Andrew Parish**)

- John C. Seymour & Elizabeth Bouden – 19 Nov 1823 (Marriage, **St. James Parish**)

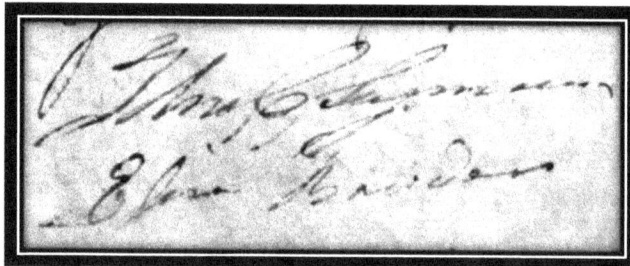

Signatures

Seymour Surname Ireland: 1600s to 1900s

- John Crossby Seymour & Unknown

  - Catherine Seymour – b. 1803, & William Minchin, b. 1790 – 10 Apr 1845 (Marriage, **St. Peter Parish**)

Signatures:

Catherine Seymour (daughter):

    Residence - 51 Lower Baggot Street - April 10, 1845

    Age at Marriage - 42 years

William Minchin, son of William Minchin (son-in-law):

    Residence - 54 Lower Baggot Street - April 10, 1845

    Occupation - Clergyman - April 10, 1845

    Age at Marriage - 55 years

    Relationship Status at Marriage - widow

William Minchin (father):

    Occupation - Esquire

John Crossby (father):

    Occupation - Clergyman

Hurst

Wedding Witnesses:

J. C. Seymour & H. G. Grady

Signatures:

- ○ John Crossby Seymour & Harriett Eccles – 11 Oct 1877 (Marriage, **St. Peter Parish**)

Signature:

Signatures (Marriage):

John Crossby Seymour (son):

Residence - Victoria House, Kingston - October 11, 1877

Occupation - Captain R N - October 11, 1877

Relationship Status at Marriage - widow

Harriett Eccles, daughter of Cuthbert Eccles (daughter-in-law):

Residence - 5 Clyde Road - October 11, 1877

Cuthbert Eccles (father):

Occupation - Gentleman

Seymour Surname Ireland: 1600s to 1900s

John Crossby Seymour (father):

Occupation - Clerk in Holy Orders

Wedding Witnesses:

Hugh Eccles & Edward Seymour

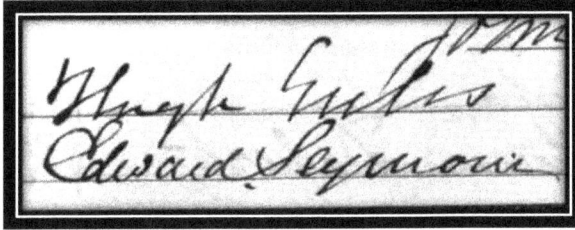

Signatures:

- John Crossly Seymour & Frances Mary Seymour – 16 May 1818 (Marriage, **St. Peter Parish**)

  - John Hogarth Seymour – b. 9 Feb 1819, bapt. 25 Feb 1819 (Baptism, **St. Peter Parish**)

  - John Hogarth Seymour – b. 31 Aug 1823, bapt. 30 Sep 1823 (Baptism, **St. Peter Parish**)

John Crossly Seymour (father):

Occupation - Lieutenant - May 16, 1818

Wedding Witnesses:

J. Seymour & E. W. Seymour

- Joseph Seymour & E. Margaret O'Neil

  - Ellen Susan Seymour – bapt. 3 Jan 1841 (Baptism, **Cork - SS. Peter & Paul Parish** (RC))

  - Mary Josephine Seymour – bapt. 5 Jul 1850 (Baptism, **Cork - SS. Peter & Paul Parish** (RC))

  - Joseph Seymour – bapt. 23 May 1852 (Baptism, **Cork - SS. Peter & Paul Parish** (RC))

Hurst

- Joseph Seymour & Ellen Hickson – 5 Sep 1844 (Marriage, **Tralee Parish**)

Signatures:

Joseph Seymour (husband):

> Residence - Blennerville - September 5, 1844

Ellen Hickson (wife):

> Residence - Killorglin - September 5, 1844

- Joseph Seymour & Ellen Seymour

  - Mary Jane Seymour – b. 9 Dec 1848, bapt. 4 Feb 1849 (Baptism, **St. Peter Parish**)

Joseph Seymour (father):

> Residence - No 3 Richmond Street - February 4, 1849

> Occupation - Policeman - February 4, 1849

- Joseph Seymour & Margaret Seymour

  - Joseph Seymour – b. 10 Jan 1844, bapt. 4 Feb 1844 (Baptism, **Clontarf Parish**)

Joseph Seymour (father):

> Residence - Clontarf - February 4, 1844

> Occupation - Esquire - February 4, 1844

- Joseph Seymour & Unknown

  - William Seymour & Marcella Keogh – 10 Nov 1850 (Marriage, **St. Thomas Parish**)

Signatures:

Seymour Surname Ireland: 1600s to 1900s

William Seymour (son):

> Residence - Cumberland Street - November 10, 1850

> Occupation - Carowner - November 10, 1850

> Relationship Status at Marriage - widow

Marcella Keogh, daughter of Timothy Keogh (daughter-in-law):

> Residence - Spring Gasdart - November 10, 1850

Timothy Keogh (father):

> Occupation - Herdsman

Joseph Seymour (father):

> Occupation - Servant

- Joseph Seymour & Unknown

  o Joseph Seymour & Anne Jane Gilbert – 21 Apr 1888 (Marriage, **Leeson Park Parish**)

Signatures:

Joseph Seymour (son):

> Residence - Mayfield House, Cork - April 21, 1888

> Occupation - Lieutenant Corporal 4 Infantry Royal Irish Regiment - April 21, 1888

> Relationship Status at Marriage - widow

Anne Jane Gilbert, daughter of Richard Gilbert (daughter-in-law):

> Residence - Moygaddy Maynooth 15 Northbrook Street Leeson Park - April 21, 1888

> Occupation - Lady - April 21, 1888

Richard Gilbert (father):

Signature:

   Occupation - Gentleman Farmer

Joseph Seymour (father):

   Occupation - County Inspector R I Constabulary

Wedding Witnesses:

Richard Gilbert & William Green

Signatures:

- Joseph John Seymour & Anne Young – 14 Nov 1816 (Marriage, **Glasnevin Parish**)

Signatures:

Joseph John Seymour (husband):

   Residence - Clonfert Parish - November 14, 1816

   Professional Title - Rev.

Seymour Surname Ireland: 1600s to 1900s

Anne Young (wife):

Residence - Glasnevin - November 14, 1816

Wedding Witnesses:

George Young, Margaret Young, Robert Seymour, & Francis William Seymour

Signatures:

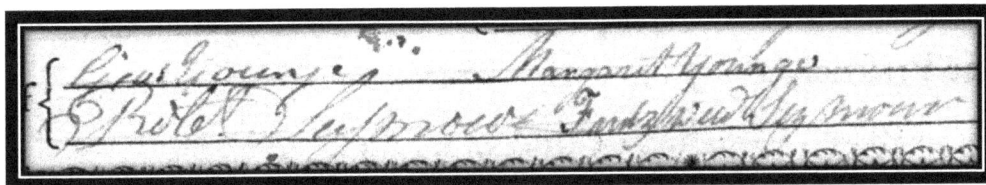

- Matthew Seymour & Eleanor Dunne

  - John Seymour – bapt. Apr 1806 (Baptism, **St. Nicholas Parish (RC)**)

- Matthew Seymour & Mary Kennedy – 29 Dec 1809 (Marriage, **St. George Parish**)

Matthew Seymour (husband):

Residence - Co. Meath - December 29, 1809

Occupation - Esquire - December 29, 1809

- Michael Seymour & Catherine O'Mahony – 9 Apr 1872 (Marriage, **Enniskeane & Desertserges Parish (RC)**)

  - Henry Joseph Seymour – bapt. 8 Jun 1873 (Baptism, **Dunmanway Parish (RC)**)

  - Joseph Daniel Seymour – b. 12 Mar 1875, bapt. 14 Mar 1875 (Baptism, **Dunmanway Parish (RC)**)

  - Margaret Mary Seymour – b. 12 Mar 1875, bapt, 14 Mar 1875 (Baptism, **Dunmanway Parish (RC)**)

- Michael Stephen Seymour & Catherine McCarthy – 3 Sep 1864 (Marriage, **Cork - South Parish (RC)**)

- Nicholas Seymour & Catherine Neil – 26 Jan 1823 (Marriage, **Bandon Parish (RC)**)

  - George Seymour – bapt. 28 Jul 1829 (Baptism, **Innishannon Parish (RC)**)

  - John Seymour – bapt. 2 Feb 1832 (Baptism, **Innishannon Parish (RC)**)

  - Nicholas Seymour – bapt. 27 Jun 1834 (Baptism, **Innishannon Parish (RC)**)

  - William Seymour – bapt. 22 Sep 1836 (Baptism, **Innishannon Parish (RC)**)

- Nicholas Seymour & Mary Unknown

  - William Seymour – bapt. 13 Feb 1774 (Baptism, **St. Mary, Pro Cathedral Parish (RC)**)

  - Elizabeth Seymour – bapt. 13 Feb 1780 (Baptism, **St. Mary, Pro Cathedral Parish (RC)**)

- Nicholas Seymour & Unknown

  - John Seymour – bapt. 10 Mar 1744, 10 Mar 1745 (Baptism, **St. Audoen Parish**)

Nicholas Seymour (father):

Social Status - poor - March 10, 1744/45

- Patrick Seymour & Mary Lyons

  - Ellen Seymour – bapt. 8 Aug 1852 (Baptism, **Cork - South Parish (RC)**)

  - Mary Seymour – bapt. 16 Jul 1854 (Baptism, **Cork - South Parish (RC)**)

- Peter Seymour & Anne Seymour

  - Sophia Seymour – b. 24 Mar 1850, bapt. 10 Apr 1850 (Baptism, **St. Mark Parish**)

  - Robert Charles Seymour – b. 6 Apr 1851, bapt. 30 Apr 1851 (Baptism, **St. Mark Parish**)

Peter Seymour (father):

Residence - Sandwith Place - April 10, 1850

Cumberland Street - April 30, 1851

Occupation - Servant - April 10, 1850

April 30, 1851

- Peter Seymour & Mary Johnstone

  - Peter Seymour – b. 17 May 1870, bapt. 15 Jun 1870 (Baptism, **St. Mary, Pro Cathedral Parish (RC)**)

Peter Seymour (father):

Residence - 11 Marlborough Street - June 15, 1870

- Peter Seymour & Mary Sweeny

  - Catherine Seymour – bapt. 3 Jan 1837 (Baptism, **Kilbrittain Parish (RC)**)

Seymour Surname Ireland: 1600s to 1900s

- Ralph Seymour & Mary Seymour

  - Robert Seymour – bur. 28 Apr 1722 (Burial, **St. Mary Parish**)

- Richard Seymour & Anne Ellen Dixon

  - John Seymour – bapt. 30 Jan 1825 (Baptism, **Cork - South Parish** (RC))

  - Joseph Seymour – bapt. 22 Jul 1827 (Baptism, **Cork - South Parish** (RC))

  - Elizabeth Seymour – bapt. 18 Apr 1830 (Baptism, **Cork - South Parish** (RC))

  - Dixon Theophilus Seymour – bapt. 5 Aug 1838 (Baptism, **Cork - South Parish** (RC))

- Richard Seymour & Julia Walsh – 25 Jan 1851 (Marriage, **Cork - South Parish** (RC))

- Richard Seymour & Mary McCarthy

  - Richard Seymour – bapt. 16 Dec 1845 (Baptism, **Cork - South Parish** (RC))

- Richard Seymour & Unknown

  - Mary Seymour – bapt. 19 Apr 1697 (Baptism, **St. Nicholas Within Parish**), bur. 24 Nov 1697

    (Burial, **St. Nicholas Within Parish**)

- Robert Seymour & Ellen Brown

  - Anne Mary Seymour – bapt. 15 Jan 1854 (Baptism, **Cork - South Parish** (RC))

  - Robert Seymour – bapt. 3 Jul 1855 (Baptism, **Cork - South Parish** (RC))

- Robert Seymour & Grissell Seymour

  - Grace Seymour – bapt. 18 Sep 1664 (Baptism, **St. Michan Parish**)

- Robert Seymour & Jane Mary Unknown

  - Robert Seymour – b. 17 Feb 1897, bapt. 31 Mar 1897 (Baptism, **St. James Parish**)

Robert Seymour (father):

Residence - People's Garden, Dublin - March 31, 1897

Occupation - Gardener - March 31, 1897

- Robert Seymour & Margaret Byrne (B y r n e)

  - Francis Joseph Seymour – b. 4 Feb 1888, bapt. 29 Sep 1893 (Baptism, **Harrington Street Parish (RC)**)

Robert Seymour (father):

  Residence - 1 Kingsland Park Avenue South Circular Road - September 29, 1893

- Robert Seymour & Margaret Seymour

  - Frank Henry Seymour – b. 4 May 1888, bapt. 1 Jul 1888 (Baptism, **Arbour Hill Barracks Parish**)

Robert Seymour (father):

  Residence - Ashgrove Cottage Palmerstown Park - July 1, 1888

  Occupation - Gunner B. A. Portobello - July 1, 1888

- Robert Seymour & Susannah Seymour

  - Jane Seymour – bur. 24 Jan 1687 (Burial, **St. Audoen Parish**)

  - Mary Seymour – bur. 2 Mar 1687 (Burial, **St. Audoen Parish**)

  - Jane Seymour – b. 21 Jun 1687, bapt. 3 Jul 1687 (Baptism, **St. Audoen Parish**)

- Robert Butson Seymour & Unknown

  - Anne Marion Sarah Seymour & James Treanor – 13 Aug 1874 (Marriage, **St. Matthias Parish**)

Signatures:

Anne Marian Sara Seymour (daughter):

  Residence - 10 Adelaide Road - August 13, 1874

James Treanor, son of William Treanor (son-in-law):

  Residence - Athenny, Galway - August 13, 1874

  Occupation - Clerk in Holy Orders - August 13, 1874

Seymour Surname Ireland: 1600s to 1900s

William Treanor (father):

　Occupation - Gentleman

Robert Butson Seymour (father):

　Occupation - Gentleman

Wedding Witnesses:

Thomas Berry & William Treanor

Signatures:

- Samuel Seymour & Bridget Unknown

  - Rebecca Seymour – bapt. 17 Mar 1754 (Baptism, **St. Michan Parish** (RC))

- Samuel Seymour & Margaret Fahey

  - Samuel Seymour – bapt. 16 Oct 1819 (Baptism, **Bandon Parish** (RC))

- Simon Mayes Seymour & Unknown

  - Edward Hugh Mayes Seymour & Eva Donovan – 15 Nov 1884 (Marriage, **St. Thomas Parish**)

Signatures:

  - Laura Beatrice Seymour – b. 2 Jun 1886, bapt. 19 Sep 1886 (Baptism, **St. Paul Parish**)

  - Eva Mary Mayes Seymour – b. 23 Jun 1888, bapt. 21 Oct 1888 (Baptism, **St. Paul Parish**)

  - Edward Hugh Seymour – b. 4 Sep 1890, bapt. 2 Nov 1890 (Baptism, **St. Paul Parish**)

Hurst

- Richard Henry Seymour – b. 14 Nov 1892, bapt. 1 Feb 1893 (Baptism, **St. Paul Parish**)

- Violet Anne May Seymour – b. 28 Dec 1894, bapt. 15 May 1895 (Baptism, **St. George Parish**)

- Arthur William Stephen – b. 26 Dec 1899, bapt. 15 Aug 1900 (Baptism, **St. Paul Parish**)

Edward Seymour (son):

Residence - No 5 St. Bridget Avenue - November 15, 1884

75 Prussia Street - September 19, 1886

R J C Cottages - October 21, 1888

R I C Cottages Phoenix Park - November 2, 1890

R I C Quarters - February 1, 1893

Phoenix Park - May 15, 1894

R N Depot - August 15, 1900

Occupation - Musician - November 15, 1884

October 21, 1888

R J C - September 19, 1886

Constable R I C - November 2, 1890

Constable - February 1, 1893

Bandsman R I C - May 15, 1894

R I C - August 15, 1900

Eva Donovan, daughter of Edwin Alexander Donovan (daughter-in-law):

Residence - St. Thomas Parish - November 15, 1884

Edwin Alexander Donovan (father):

Signature:

Occupation - Gentleman

Simon Mayes Seymour (father):

Occupation - Officer in the Army

Wedding Witnesses:

E. A. Donovan & Maud Donovan

Signatures:

- Simion Robert E. Seymour & Unknown

  o Anne Elizabeth Matilda Seymour & Richard Kellett – 15 Dec 1857 (Marriage, **St. Mary Parish**)

Signatures:

Anne Elizabeth Matilda Seymour (daughter):

Residence - **27 Upper Dorset Street** - December 15, 1857

Richard Kellett, son of Lawrence Kellett (son-in-law):

Residence - Bridgesford House, Co. Meath - December 15, 1857

Occupation - Gentleman - December 15, 1857

Relationship Status at Marriage - widow

Lawrence Kellett (father):

Occupation - Gentleman

Simion Robert E. Seymour (father):

Occupation - Gentleman

Hurst

- Smith Francis Seymour & Unknown

  o Albinia Seymour & Charles W. Russell – 16 Jul 1863 (Marriage, **Chapelizod Parish**)

Albinia Seymour (daughter):

Residence - Chapelizod - July 16, 1863

Charles W. Russell, son of James Russell (son-in-law):

Residence - 18 Percy Place, Dublin - July 16, 1863

Occupation - Education Office - July 16, 1863

James Russell (father):

Occupation - Solicitor

Smith Francis Seymour (father):

Occupation - Gentleman

- Stanley Seymour & Jane Osborne (O s b o r n e) – 5 Oct 1726 (Marriage, **St. Anne Parish**)

  o William Seymour – bapt. 4 Oct 1727 (Baptism, **St. Catherine Parish**), bur. 29 Jan 1729 (Burial, **St. Catherine Parish**)

- Stanley Seymour & Susanna Seymour

  o Esther Seymour – bapt. 16 Jul 1732 (Baptism, **St. Catherine Parish**)

- Thomas Seymour & Mary Maloney – 24 Jul 1853 (Marriage, **St. Andrew Parish** (RC))

  o Mary Seymour – b. 1854, bapt. 1854 (Baptism, **St. Andrew Parish** (RC))

  o Thomas Seymour – b. 1855, bapt. 1855 (Baptism, **St. Andrew Parish** (RC))

  o John Seymour – b. 1857, bapt. 1857 (Baptism, **St. Andrew Parish** (RC))

  o Thomas Christopher – b. 1860, bapt. 1860 (Baptism, **St. Andrew Parish** (RC))

Thomas Seymour (father):

Residence - 10 Baggot Court - 1860

Seymour Surname Ireland: 1600s to 1900s

- Thomas Seymour & Matilda Lawrence – 5 Jul 1822 (Marriage, **St. George Parish**)

Signatures:

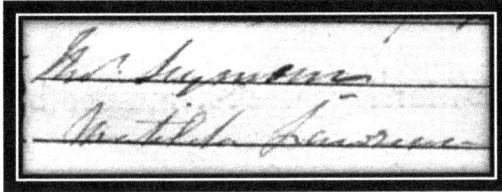

o Matilda Margaret Seymour & Henry Blake Mahon – 20 Dec 1859 (Marriage, **St. Peter Parish**)

Signatures:

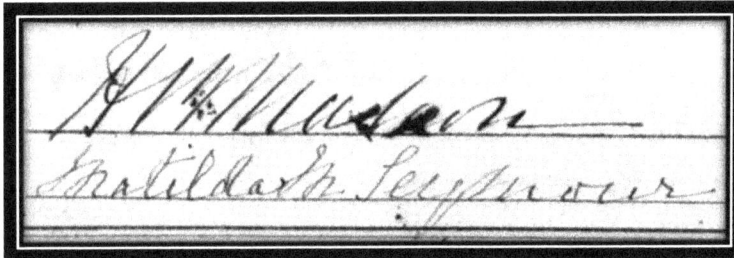

Matilda Margaret Seymour (daughter):

Residence - 34 Lower Baggot Street - December 20, 1859

Henry Blake Mahon, son of Thomas Mahon (son-in-law):

Residence - Monivea Athemy, Co. Galway - December 20, 1859

Occupation - Esquire - December 20, 1859

Thomas Mahon (father):

Occupation - Major Galway Militia

Thomas Seymour (father):

Occupation - Captain Galway Militia

Hurst

o   Walter Seymour & Belinda Jane Dunbar Gordon – 20 Dec 1859 (Marriage, **St. Peter Parish**)

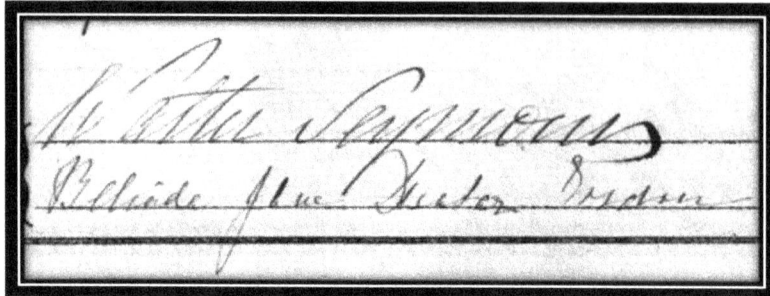

Signatures:

- Belinda Jane Seymour – b. 12 Oct 1862, bapt. 17 Oct 1862 (Baptism, **St. Stephen Parish**)

Walter Seymour (son):

Residence - Ballymore Castle, Co. Galway - December 20, 1859

Ballymore Castle Ballinasloe - October 17, 1862

Occupation - Esquire - December 20, 1859

October 17, 1862

Belinda Jane Dunbar Gordon, daughter of Abercrombie Gordon (daughter-in-law):

Residence - 64 Fitzwilliam Square North - December 20, 1859

Abercrombie Gordon (father):

Occupation - Clerk in Holy Orders

Thomas Seymour (father):

Residence - Clonfert, Co. Galway - July 5, 1822

Occupation - Esquire - July 5, 1822

Captain Galway Militia

Matilda Lawrence (mother):

Residence - St. George Parish - July 5, 1822

- Thomas Seymour & Sarah Seymour

  o Patrick Seymour & Christine Cosgrave – 6 Apr 1858 (Marriage, **St. Mary, Pro Cathedral Parish**

  (RC))

Patrick Seymour (son):

  Residence - 10 Langrish Place - April 6, 1858

Christine Cosgrave, daughter of Dionysius Cosgrave & Catherine Cosgrave

(daughter-in-law):

  Residence - 10 Langrish Place - April 6, 1858

- Thomas Seymour & Unknown

  o Henry Seymour & Elizabeth Thompson – 1 Sep 1877 (Marriage, **St. Peter Parish**)

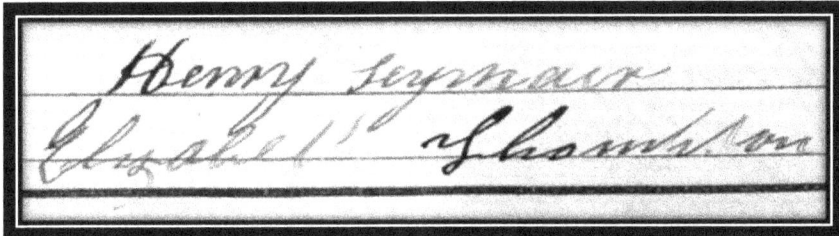

Signatures:

Henry Seymour (son):

  Residence - Abbeyliex, Queens County - September 1, 1877

  Occupation - Coachman - September 1, 1877

Elizabeth Thompson, daughter of Thomas Thompson (daughter-in-law):

  Residence - 4 Albert Place off Charlemont Street - September 1, 1877

Thomas Thompson (father):

  Occupation - Carpenter

Thomas Seymour (father):

  Occupation - Butcher

Hurst

- Timothy Seymour & Juliana Seymour

  o Marcella Seymour & James Magurk – 24 Oct 1858 (Marriage, **St. Mary, Pro Cathedral Parish (RC)**)

Marcella Seymour (daughter):

Residence - 20 Summer Place - October 24, 1858

James Magurk, son of Edward Magurk & Dorah Magurk (son-in-law):

Residence - 6 Poole Street - October 24, 1858

- Walter Seymour & Catherine Unknown

  o Patrick Seymour – bapt. 20 Jan 1805 (Baptism, **St. Mary, Pro Cathedral Parish (RC)**)

- William Seymour & Bridget Kinsella – 8 Jun 1851 (Marriage, **St. Andrew Parish (RC)**)

  o Elizabeth Seymour – b. 1852, bapt. 1852 (Baptism, **St. Andrew Parish (RC)**)

  o William Seymour – b. 1854, bapt. 1854 (Baptism, **St. Andrew Parish (RC)**)

  o Sarah Seymour – b. 23 May 1861, bapt. 5 Jun 1861 (Baptism, **St. Mary, Pro Cathedral Parish (RC)**)

William Seymour (father):

Residence - 20 Summer Place - June 5, 1861

- William Seymour & Catherine Bomer – 2 Apr 1840 (Marriage, **St. Paul Parish**)

- William Seymour & Catherine Unknown

  o Garret Seymour – bapt. 15 Nov 1803 (Baptism, **St. Mary, Pro Cathedral Parish (RC)**)

  o James Seymour – bapt. 14 Dec 1806 (Baptism, **St. Mary, Pro Cathedral Parish (RC)**)

Seymour Surname Ireland: 1600s to 1900s

- William Seymour & Elizabeth Savage – 18 Jun 1827 (Marriage, **St. George Parish**)

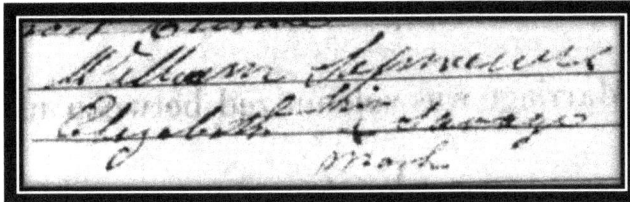

Signatures:

William Seymour (husband):

    Residence - St. George Parish - June 18, 1827

    Occupation - Servant to Mr. Euster - June 18, 1827

Elizabeth Savage (wife):

    Residence - St. George Parish - June 18, 1827

- William Seymour & Elizabeth Seymour

  - James Seymour – bapt. 18 Mar 1792 (Baptism, **St. Mary Parish**)

William Seymour (father):

    Residence - Tuckers Row - March 18, 1792

- William Seymour & Elizabeth Unknown

  - George Seymour – b. 2 Feb 1825, bapt. 30 Mar 1825 (Baptism, **St. Peter Parish**)

- William Seymour & Judith Unknown

  - Judith Seymour – bapt. 15 Jun 1751 (Baptism, **St. John Parish**)

Hurst

- William Seymour & Marcella Murphy

  - Bridget Mary Seymour, bapt. 1 Feb 1856 (Baptism, **St. Audoen Parish (RC)**) & Edward Connor – 20 Jun 1886 (Marriage, **St. Mary, Pro Cathedral Parish (RC)**)

    - Anne Connor – b. 9 Feb 1888, bapt. 13 Feb 1888 (Baptism, **St. Mary, Pro Cathedral Parish (RC)**)

    - Mary Jane Connor – b. 15 Feb 1890, bapt. 17 Feb 1890 (Baptism, **St. Mary, Pro Cathedral Parish (RC)**)

    - Michael Connor – b. 4 Jun 1897, bapt. 6 Jun 1897 (Baptism, **St. Mary, Pro Cathedral Parish (RC)**)

Bridget Seymour (daughter):

Residence - 34 Upper Gloucester Street - June 20, 1886

Edward Connor, son of Edward Connor & Anne Ryan (son-in-law):

Residence - 153 Townsend Street - June 20, 1886

34 Upper Gloucester Street - February 13, 1888

February 17, 1890

11 Frederick Court - June 6, 1897

- William Seymour & Margaret Seymour

  - John Seymour – bapt. 3 Jan 1738 (Baptism, **St. Audoen Parish**)

- William Seymour & Mary Lawlor

  - Patrick Seymour – bapt. 20 Jan 1813 (Baptism, **St. Catherine Parish (RC)**)

- William Seymour & Mary Seymour

  - Richard Seymour – b. 13 Mar 1856, bapt. 16 Mar 1856 (Baptism, **St. Mary Parish**)

William Seymour (father):

Residence - 43 Henry Street - March 16, 1856

Occupation - Porter - March 16, 1856

Seymour Surname Ireland: 1600s to 1900s

- William Seymour & Mary Unknown

  o Richard Seymour & Louisa Murphy – 7 Feb 1875 (Marriage, **St. Andrew Parish (RC)**)

Richard Seymour (son):

  Residence - 107 Great Britain Street - February 7, 1875

Louisa Murphy, daughter of John Murphy & Louisa Unknown (daughter-in-law):

  Residence - 6 D'Olier Street - February 7, 1875

- William Seymour & Mary Jane Seymour

  o Emily Seymour – bapt. 1 Jun 1851 (Baptism, **Arbour Hill Barracks Parish**)

William Seymour (father):

  Residence - Linen Hall Barracks - June 1, 1851

  Occupation - Corporal Band 14th Foot - June 1, 1851

- William Seymour & Unknown

  o Mary Anne Seymour & Edward Hendrick – 2 Jan 1848 (Marriage, **St. Mary Parish**)

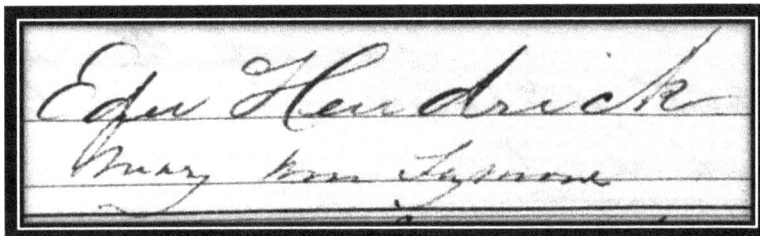

Signatures:

Mary Anne Seymour (daughter):

  Residence - 32 Capel Street - January 2, 1848

Edward Hendrick, son of Peter Hendrick (son-in-law):

  Residence - 32 Capel Street - January 2, 1848

  Occupation - Druggist - January 2, 1848

Peter Hendrick (father):

  Occupation - Gentleman

William Seymour (father):

  Occupation - Gentleman

Hurst

- William George Seymour & Ellen Dalton

  o Richard Dalton Seymour, b. 1 Sep 1870, bapt. 4 Sep 1870 (Baptism, **Rotunda Chapel Parish**) (Baptism, **St. Mary Parish**) & Sarah Frances Harris – 12 Aug 1896 (Marriage, **North Strand Parish**)

Signatures:

Richard Dalton Seymour (husband):

   Residence - 94 North Strand Road - August 12, 1896

   Occupation - Commercial Manager - August 12, 1896

Sarah Frances Harris, daughter of David John Wellesley Pole Harris (daughter-in-law):

   Residence - 7 Waterloo Avenue - August 12, 1896

David John Wellesley Pole Harris (father):

   Occupation - Commercial [Traveller]

William George Seymour (father):

   Occupation - Commercial Manager

Wedding Witnesses:

David C. Harris & William Wellesley Harris

Signatures:

Seymour Surname Ireland: 1600s to 1900s

o   William Henry Seymour – b. 30 Nov 1872, bapt. 8 Dec 1872 (Baptism, **Rotunda Chapel Parish**)

o   Edward Mayne Seymour – bapt. 8 Nov 1874 (Baptism, **Rotunda Chapel Parish**)

William George Seymour (father):

Residence - 4 Frankfort Terrace - September 4, 1870

5 Wesley Place - December 8, 1872

111 Leinster Road - November 8, 1874

Occupation - Assist in Iron Store - September 4, 1870

Ironmonger - December 8, 1872

Individual Births/Baptisms

- Alicia Seymour – bapt. 8 Feb 1869 (Baptism, **SS. Michael & John Parish** (RC))

Alicia Seymour (child):

    Residence - 37 Castle Street - February 8, 1869

- Charlotte Seymour – b. 24 Mar 1863, bapt. 29 Mar 1863 (Baptism, **Rotunda Chapel Parish**)

- Elizabeth Seymour – bapt. 20 Jun 1838 (Baptism, **St. Paul Parish**)

- John Seymour – bapt. 20 Jun 1838 (Baptism, **St. Paul Parish**)

Individual Burials

- Anne Seymour – bur. 17 Jun 1709 (Burial, **St. Catherine Parish**)

- Anne Seymour – bur. 11 Jun 1745 (Burial, **St. Paul Parish**)

- Bartholomew Seymour – b. 1769, 19 Jun 1819 (Burial, **St. Mark Parish**)

Bartholomew Seymour (deceased):

    Residence - St. Andrew Parish - Before June 19, 1819

    Age at Death - 50 years

- Bridget Seymour – bur. 10 Jan 1769 (Burial, **St. James Parish**)

Bridget Seymour (deceased):

    Residence - New Market - Before January 10, 1769

- Elizabeth Seymour – b. Apr 1829, bur. 22 Jan 1830 (Burial, **St. Mark Parish**)

Elizabeth Seymour (deceased):

    Residence - Townsend Street - Before January 22, 1830

    Age at Death - 9 months

- Ellen Seymour – b. 1822, d. 26 Aug 1867, bur. 26 Aug 1867 (Burial, **Kilcolman Parish**)

Ellen Seymour (deceased):

    Residence - Killorglin - August 26, 1867

    Age at Death - 45 years

- Frances Seymour – bur. 31 Oct 1821 (Burial, **Irishtown Parish**)

- George Seymour – b. Jan 1879, bur. 14 Feb 1879 (Burial, **St. Peter Parish**)

George Seymour (deceased):

    Residence - 90 Heytesbury Street - Before February 14, 1879

    Age at Death - 6 weeks

- Georgina Pagst Seymour – b. 1881, d. 6 Sep 1882, bur. 1882 (Burial, **St. Peter Parish**)

Georgina PAgst Seymour (deceased):

> **Residence - 16 Ely Place - Before September 6, 1882**

> **Age at Death - 1 year**

- Hannah Seymour – bur. 20 Sep 1762 (Burial, **St. Paul Parish**)

- Hannah Seymour – b. 1813, bur. 7 Aug 1816 (Burial, **St. Peter Parish**)

Hannah Seymour (deceased):

> **Residence - Mountague Street - Before August 7, 1816**

- Jane Seymour – b. 1849, bur. 17 Feb 1851 (Burial, **St. Peter Parish**)

Jane Seymour (deceased):

> **Residence - Kevin Street - Before February 17, 1851**

> **Age at Death - 2 years**

- John Seymour – bur. 28 Apr 1665 (Burial, **St. John Parish**)

John Seymour (deceased):

> **Occupation - Soldier - April 28, 1665**

- John Seymour – bur. 13 Oct 1695 (Burial, **St. Nicholas Without Parish**)

John Seymour (deceased):

> **Residence - Patrick Street - Before October 13, 1695**

- John Seymour (Child) – bur. 10 Nov 1722 (Burial, **St. Catherine Parish**)

- John Seymour – bur. 25 Mar 1819 (Burial, **Irishtown Parish**)

- John A. Seymour – b. 1799, bur. 30 Nov 1821 (Burial, **St. Peter Parish**)

John A. Seymour (deceased):

> **Residence - Ranelagh - Before November 30, 1821**

> **Age at Death - 22 years**

> **Place of Burial - St. Kevin's Church Yard**

- Jon Seymour – bur. 28 Oct 1733 (Burial, **St. Paul Parish**)

- Jzman Seymour – bur. 2 Jul 1690 (Burial, **St. Nicholas Without Parish**)

Seymour Surname Ireland: 1600s to 1900s

- Margaret Seymour – bur. 19 Oct 1739 (Burial, **St. Catherine Parish**)

- Mary Seymour – bur. 8 Jun 1670 (Burial, **St. John Parish**)

- Mary Seymour – bur. 24 Nov 1697 (Burial, **St. Nicholas Without Parish**)

- Mary Seymour – bur. 18 Aug 1734 (Burial, **St. Mary Parish**)

- Mary Seymour – bur. 12 Feb 1802 (Burial, **St. John Parish**)

Mary Seymour (deceased):

    Residence - Virginia Court - Before February 12, 1802

- Mary Seymour – bur. 19 Jul 1806 (Burial, **St. James Parish**)

Mary Seymour (deceased):

    Residence - Abbey Street - Before July 19, 1806

- Mary Anne Seymour – bur. 7 Jan 1819 (Burial, **St. James Parish**)

Mary Anne Seymour (deceased):

    Residence - Henry Street - January 7, 1819

- Matthew Seymour – bur. 5 Nov 1819 (Burial, **Irishtown Parish**)

- Richard Seymour – bur. 21 Jul 1729 (Burial, **St. Nicholas Without Parish**)

Richard Seymour (deceased):

    Residence - New Street - July 21, 1729

- Robert Seymour – b. Apr 1851, bur. 25 Aug 1851 (Burial, **St. Catherine Parish**)

Robert Seymour (deceased):

    Residence - Cork Street - Before August 25, 1851

    Age at Death - 5 months

- Robert Martin Seymour – bur. 27 Mar 1775 (Burial, **St. Paul Parish**)

Robert Martin Seymour (deceased):

    Occupation - Captain, 10th Regiment

Hurst

- Sophia Seymour – b. Apr 1850, bur. 28 Sep 1850 (Burial, **St. Catherine Parish**)

Sophia Seymour (deceased):

> **Residence - Ardee Street - Before September 28, 1850**
>
> **Age at Death - 6 months**

- Thomas Seymour – bur. 20 Aug 1694 (Burial, **St. Michan Parish**)

- William Seymour – b. 1698, bur. 23 Mar 1746 (Burial, **St. Werburgh Parish**)

William Seymour (deceased):

> **Residence - Essex Street - Before March 23, 1746**
>
> **Age at Death - 48 years**
>
> **Cause of Death - decay**

Individual Marriages

- Alicia Seymour & Charles Humphries – 22 Nov 1812 (Marriage, **St. Mary Parish**)

- Anne Seymour & Bartholomew Archbold

  - Patrick Gulielmo Archbold – bapt. 27 Apr 1831 (Baptism, **St. Michan Parish** (RC))

- Anne Seymour & Patrick Moran – 17 Aug 1847 (Marriage, **St. Andrew Parish** (RC))

  - Thomas Moran – b. 1852, bapt. 1852 (Baptism, **St. Andrew Parish** (RC))

  - Julia Charlotte Moran – b. 1859, bapt. 1859 (Baptism, **St. Andrew Parish** (RC))

  - Patrick William Moran – b. 1861, bapt. 1861 (Baptism, **St. Andrew Parish** (RC))

  - George Moran – b. 1863, bapt. 1863 (Baptism, **St. Andrew Parish** (RC))

  - Alfred George Moran – b. 1865, bapt. 1865 (Baptism, **St. Andrew Parish** (RC))

  - Bartholomew William Moran – b. 1867, bapt. 1867 (Baptism, **St. Andrew Parish** (RC))

  - Mary Moran & Matthew Clancy – 7 May 1871 (Marriage, **Harrington Street Parish** (RC))

Mary Moran (daughter):

  Residence - **29 Cuff Street** - May 7, 1871

Matthew Clancy, son of Stephen Clancy & Rebecca Valentine (son-in-law):

  Residence - **50 York Street** - May 7, 1871

Patrick Moran (father):

  Residence - **5 Fitzwilliam Lane** - 1859

  1861

  1865

  1867

  Fitzwilliam Lane - 1863

- Catherine Seymour & Francis Burke – 24 Jun 1849 (Marriage, **St. Mary, Pro Cathedral Parish** (RC))

- Catherine Seymour & John Lamond – 10 Feb 1841 (Marriage, **St. Mary Parish**)

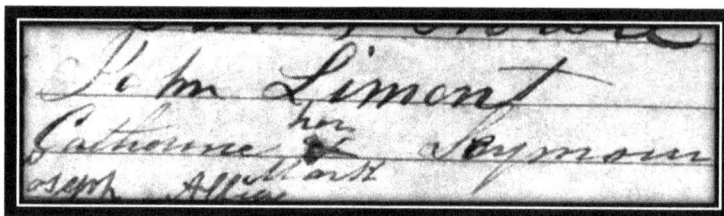

Signatures:

- Catherine Seymour & John Murtha

  o Mary Anne Murtha – bapt. 23 Jun 1845 (Baptism, **St. Michan Parish (RC)**)

- Catherine Seymour & William Doherty

  o Christopher Doherty – b. 4 Apr 1892, bapt. 31 May 1895 (Baptism, **St. Mary, Pro Cathedral Parish (RC)**)

William Doherty (father):

  Residence - 3 Gardiner's Lane - May 31, 1895

- Catherine Isabel Seymour & Robert Henry Persse – 16 Mar 1828 (Marriage, **St. George Parish**)

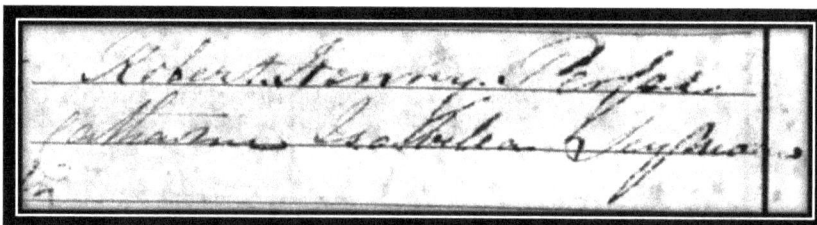

Signatures:

Catherine Isabel Seymour (wife):

  Residence - St. George Parish - March 16, 1828

Robert Henry Persse (husband):

  Residence - Killinan, Co. Galway - March 16, 1828

  Occupation - Esquire - March 16, 1828

Seymour Surname Ireland: 1600s to 1900s

Wedding Witnesses:

Burton Persse & Henry Torrens Graham

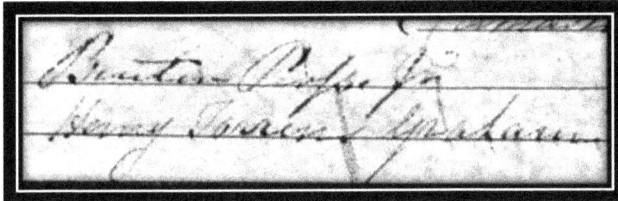

Signatures:

- Eleanor Seymour & Daniel Leeson

  o Gulielmo Leeson – bapt. 1769 (Baptism, **St. Andrew Parish (RC)**)

- Elizabeth Seymour & Bartholomew Short

  o Emily Short – bapt. 7 Jun 1818 (Baptism, **SS. Michael & John Parish (RC)**)

- Elizabeth Seymour & John Gold Dease – 24 Jun 1849 (Marriage, **Cork - SS. Peter & Paul Parish (RC)**)

- Elizabeth Seymour & John Thomas Ribbons

  o John Thomas Ribbons & Bridget Tierney (T i e r n e y) – 4 Mar 1889 (Marriage, **Rathmines Parish**

  (RC))

John Thomas Ribbons (son):

   Residence - 1 Walkers Cottages - March 4, 1889

Bridget Tierney, daughter of Michael Tierney & Anne Connor (daughter-in-law):

   Residence - 15 Temple Place - March 4, 1889

- Elizabeth Seymour & Peter Burnett (B u r n e t t) – 1 Jan 1714 (Marriage, **St. Bride Parish**)

- Elizabeth Seymour & Robert Murphy

  o John Murphy – bapt. 1 Jan 1866 (Baptism, **Cork - South Parish (RC)**)

  o Eleanor Murphy – bapt. 3 Jul 1868 (Baptism, **Cork - South Parish (RC)**)

  o Joan Murphy – bapt. 22 Aug 1870 (Baptism, **Cork - South Parish (RC)**)

Hurst

- Elizabeth Grace Seymour & Timothy Moynihan

  - Frederick Henry Moynihan – b. 31 Jan 1864, bapt. 14 Feb 1864 (Baptism, **Cork - SS. Peter & Paul Parish** (RC))

  - Elizabeth Jane Moynihan – b. 6 Apr 1866, bapt. 6 May 1866 (Baptism, **Cork - SS. Peter & Paul Parish** (RC))

- Ellen Seymour & John Crane

  - John Crane – bapt. 10 Aug 1817 (Baptism, **Cork - South Parish** (RC))

- Ellen Seymour & John Lawlor – 1 May 1792 (Marriage, **Tralee Parish** (RC))

  - Jane Lawlor – b. 13 Nov 1806, bapt. 13 Nov 1806 (Baptism, **Tralee Parish** (RC))

John Lawlor (father):

Residence - Tralee - November 13, 1806

- Ellen Seymour & Joseph Coppinger

  - Elizabeth Coppinger – bapt. 3 Mar 1827 (Baptism, **Cork - SS. Peter & Paul Parish** (RC))

- Fanny Seymour & James Crowly

  - Daniel Crowly – bapt. 10 Jan 1826 (Baptism, **Innishannon Parish** (RC))

  - James Crowly – bapt. 10 Aug 1830 (Baptism, **Innishannon Parish** (RC))

- Frances Seymour & Joseph Thomas Kane – 20 Nov 1816 (Marriage, **St. Peter Parish**)

  - Joseph Seymour Kane – b. 13 Jul 1819, bapt. 29 Jul 1819 (Baptism, **St. Peter Parish**)

- Jane Seymour & Daniel McCarthy

  - Daniel McCarthy – b. 19 Dec 1805, bapt. 19 Dec 1805 (Baptism, **Tralee Parish** (RC))

Daniel McCarthy (father):

Residence - Tralee - December 19, 1805

- Jane Seymour & J. Fitzpatrick

  - Gulielmo Matthew Fitzpatrick – bapt. 3 Jan 1826 (Baptism, **Rathmines Parish** (RC))

Seymour Surname Ireland: 1600s to 1900s

- Jane Seymour & James Russell

  o Michael Russell – bapt. 1 Mar 1865 (Baptism, Tracton Abbey Parish (RC))

- Jane Seymour & Patrick John Quinn

  o John Quinn – bapt. 24 Mar 1822 (Baptism, St. Michan Parish (RC))

- Jane Seymour & Samuel Tarrant

  o Richard Stephen Tarrant – bapt. 29 Dec 1844 (Baptism, Cork - South Parish (RC))

  o Ellen Tarrant – bapt. 4 Nov 1848 (Baptism, Cork - South Parish (RC))

  o Samuel Tarrant – bapt. 3 May 1851 (Baptism, Cork - South Parish (RC))

  o James Tarrant – bapt. 23 Apr 1854 (Baptism, Cork - South Parish (RC))

  o Samuel Joseph Tarrant – bapt. 21 Jun 1856 (Baptism, Cork - South Parish (RC))

- Jane Seymour & Timothy Rielly

  o James Rielly – bapt. 25 Dec 1848 (Baptism, Cork - South Parish (RC))

- Joan Seymour & Samuel Forrest

  o Anne Forrest – bapt. 31 Jan 1847 (Baptism, Cork - South Parish (RC))

  o John Forrest – bapt. 28 Jun 1852 (Baptism, Cork - South Parish (RC))

- Julia Seymour & Michael Thompson – 15 Feb 1868 (Marriage, Cork - SS. Peter & Paul Parish (RC))

  o Mary Bridget Thompson – b. 31 May 1868, bapt. 14 Jun 1868 (Baptism, Cork - SS. Peter & Paul Parish (RC))

  o William Thompson – b. 2 Mar 1872, bapt. 17 Mar 1872 (Baptism, Cork - SS. Peter & Paul Parish (RC))

Julia Seymour (mother):
    Residence - 13 Brown Street - February 15, 1868
Michael Thompson (father):
    Residence - 2 Fishamble Lane - February 15, 1868

- Honora Seymour & Timothy Hegarthy

  - John Hegarthy – bapt. 21 Jun 1853 (Baptism, **Castlehaven & Myross Parish** (RC))

- Honora Seymour & Timothy Reilly

  - Timothy Reilly – bapt. 21 Nov 1845 (Baptism, **Kilmichael Parish** (RC))

Timothy Reilly (father):

Residence - Mountmusic - November 21, 1845

- Louisa Seymour & Martin Campbell

  - Charles Campbell – bapt. 6 Jan 1854 (Baptism, **Rathmines Parish** (RC))

  - Henry George Campbell – b. 8 May 1857, bapt. 7 Jul 1857 (Baptism, **St. Catherine Parish** (RC))

  - John Campbell – b. 4 Jun 1859, bapt. 11 Jul 1859 (Baptism, **St. James Parish** (RC))

  - Louisa Campbell – bapt. 29 Aug 1861 (Baptism, **St. James Parish** (RC))

Martin Campbell (father):

Residence - 4 Alan Place - July 7, 1857

24 Dolphin's Barn - July 11, 1859

August 29, 1861

- Margaret Seymour & Cornelius (C o r n e l i u s) Shady – 27 Aug 1864 (Marriage, **Cork - SS. Peter & Paul Parish** (RC))

Margaret Seymour (wife):

Residence - 8 Patrick Street - August 27, 1864

Cornelius Shady (husband):

Residence - Clorneen - August 27, 1864

- Margaret Seymour & Dennis McCarthy – 26 Jan 1839 (Marriage, **Enniskeane & Desertserges Parish** (RC))

- Margaret Seymour & Edward Wight

  - Catherine Frances Wight – b. 1824, bapt. 1824 (Baptism, **St. Peter Parish**)

  - John Wight – b. 1825, bapt. 1825 (Baptism, **St. Peter Parish**)

Seymour Surname Ireland: 1600s to 1900s

- Margaret Unknown Seymour & William Willis – 8 Dec 1765 (Marriage, **St. Bride Parish**)

Margaret Unknown Seymour (wife):

　Relationship Status at Marriage - widow

William Willis (husband):

　Occupation - Gentleman - December 8, 1765

- Margaret Seymour & Michael Cullen – 23 Sep 1850 (Marriage, **St. Andrew Parish (RC)**)

　○　William Seymour – b. 1863, bapt. 1863 (Baptism, **St. Andrew Parish (RC)**)

　○　Christopher Cullen – b. 1867, bapt. 1867 (Baptism, **St. Andrew Parish (RC)**)

　○　John Joseph Cullen – b. 1869, bapt. 1869 (Baptism, **St. Andrew Parish (RC)**)

　○　Patrick Cullen & Elizabeth Bradley – 17 Sep 1877 (Marriage, **Rathmines Parish (RC)**)

Patrick Cullen (son):

　Residence - Stephen's Lane - September 17, 1877

Elizabeth Bradley, daughter of John Bradley & Elizabeth Bermingham (daughter-in-law):

　Residence- Dunville Terrace - September 17, 1877

Michael Cullen (father):

　Residence - 7 Verschoyle Place - 1863

　　　　15 Verschoyle Place - 1867

　　　　12 Verschoyle Place - 1869

- Mary Seymour & Cornelius (C o r n e l i u s) Creedon

　○　Cornelius (C o r n e l i u s) Creedon – bapt. 23 Jan 1810 (Baptism, **Cork - SS. Peter & Paul Parish**

　　(RC))

Cornelius Creedon (father):

　Residence - Angel Lane - January 23, 1810

- Mary Seymour & James Murphy – 16 Jun 1811 (Marriage, **St. Andrew Parish (RC)**)

- Mary Seymour & James Noonan

  o Margaret Noonan – bapt. 18 Jul 1791 (Baptism, **Cork - South Parish** (RC))

  o Mary Noonan – bapt. 6 Apr 1794 (Baptism, **Cork - South Parish** (RC))

  o William Noonan – bapt. Oct 1795 (Baptism, **Cork - SS. Peter & Paul Parish** (RC))

  o Harriet Noonan – bapt. 18 Aug 1800 (Baptism, **Cork - SS. Peter & Paul Parish** (RC))

  o John Noonan – bapt. 11 Nov 1801 (Baptism, **Cork - SS. Peter & Paul Parish** (RC))

James Noonan (father):

Residence - Christ Church Lane - July 18, 1791

Carey's Lane - October 1795

November 11, 1801

- Mary Seymour & John Doolan

  o John Doolan – b. 29 Jun 1807, bapt. 29 Jun 1807 (Baptism, **Tralee Parish** (RC))

- Mary Seymour & John Halloran

  o Jane Halloran – bapt. 29 Oct 1857 (Baptism, **Carrigaline & Templebrigid Parish** (RC))

- Mary Seymour & Patrick Reddy – 8 Aug 1769 (Baptism, **Cork - SS. Peter & Paul Parish** (RC))

- Mary Seymour & Robert Kelly

  o George Kelly – bapt. 10 Apr 1770 (Baptism, **St. Catherine Parish** (RC))

- Mary Seymour & Thomas Forrest

  o Jane Forrest – bapt.23 Jun 1817 (Baptism, **Cork - South Parish** (RC))

- Mary Anne Seymour & Robert Rundell Guinness – 2 Nov 1822 (Marriage, **St. Peter Parish**)

Mary Anne Seymour (wife):

Occupation - Spinster - November 2, 1822

Robert Rundell Guinness (husband):

Residence - Stillorgan - November 2, 1822

- Sarah Seymour & John Tuite

  o Edward Tuite & Mary Anne McCormack (M c C o r m a c k) – 6 Mar 1885 (Marriage, **Chapelizod**

    Parish (RC))

Edward Tuite (son):

  Residence - Black horse Lane - March 6, 1885

Mary Anne Mc Cormack, daughter of Gulielmo McCormack & Marion McHugh

(daughter-in-law):

  Residence - Black Horse Lane - March 6 1885

- Winifred Seymour & Patrick Nuttes – Dec 1798 (Marriage, **St. Michan Parish** (RC))

Name Variations

Includes Latin and Abbreviated forms of names found in the original documents.

Anne = Ann, Anna, Annae, Annie

Benjamin = Benjn

Catherine = Cath, Cathe, Cathne, Catharin, Catharina, Catharinae, Catharinam, Catharine, Catherin, Catherinae, Catherinam, Kate, Kathrine, Katharine, Katherine

Charles = Chas

Christine = Christina

Dorothy = Doraty

Edward = Edwardus, Edwd

Eleanor = Eleonor, Elianor, Elinor, Elnr, Ellnor, Nellie, Nora

Elizabeth = Eliz, Eliza, Elizabet, Elizth, Bessie

Frances = Frans

Francis = Fran

George = Geo, Georg

Henry = Henery, Henricus

James = Jacobi, Jacobum, Jacobus, Jas

Jane = Joanna, Joanne

John = Jno, Joannes, Joannis

Joseph = Jos, Josh

Josephine = Josephina

Margaret = Margartia, Margeret, Margarett, Margeret, Magerett, Margret, Mgt, Margt, Margtt

Mary = Maria, Mariae, Mariam

Mary Anne = Mary Ann, Maryann, Maryanne, Marian, Mariane, Mariann, Mariannae, Marianne

Seymour Surname Ireland: 1600s to 1900s

Matthew = Mat, Matt, Mathew

Michael = Michaelis, Mich, Miche, Michl, Michll

Patrick = Pat, Patt, Patk, Patricii

Richard = Richd

Robert = Robt

Teresa = Theresa

Thomas = Thos, Ths

William = Willm, Wm

Notes

Notes

Notes

Notes

Notes

Notes

Index

D

E

F

J

K

L

Hurst

Seymour Surname Ireland: 1600s to 1900s

Seymour Surname Ireland: 1600s to 1900s

Hurst

About The Author

Donovan Hurst graduated from San Diego State University with a Bachelor of Arts in the major field of studies of History and a minor in the field of studies of Anthropology. He is a current member of The General Society of Mayflower Descendants and has been conducting genealogical research for over 10 years tracing back his ancestors to their ancestral homelands in Denmark, England, France, Germany, Ireland, Norway, and Scotland.

www.ingramcontent.com/pod-product-compliance
Lightning Source LLC
Chambersburg PA
CBHW081157270326
41930CB00014B/3194